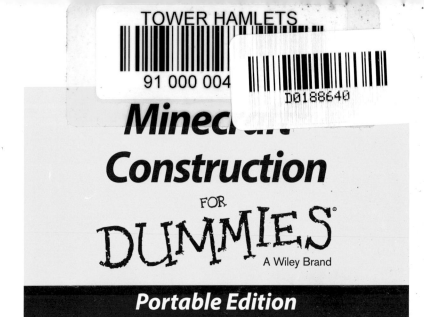

Minecraft
Construction

FOR

DUMMIES®

A Wiley Brand

Portable Edition

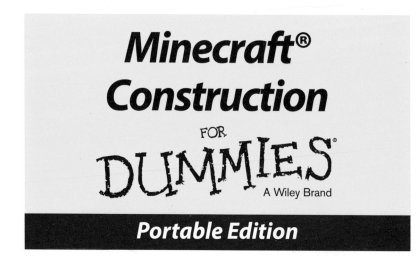

Minecraft®
Construction
FOR
DUMMIES®
A Wiley Brand

Portable Edition

by Adam Cordeiro and Emily Nelson

FOR
DUMMIES®
A Wiley Brand

Contents at a Glance

Table of Contents

Introduction

*M*inecraft is about two concepts: Destroy obstacles and create your world. When you're not mining or adventuring, for example, you can enter the limitless world of construction, to take apart the land and reconstruct it in your own way. You can create castles, gardens, bridges, factories, modern art, and many other architectural structures. Minecraft offers you so many ways to build — and so many ways to redesign your world to your liking — that it can be overwhelming to figure out how to start.

This book gives you the tools that are necessary to build everything you can envision — and to discover some possibilities that you may not have known before. You can find out how to gather necessary materials, create proper shapes and textures, and build anything you want in either Survival mode or Creative mode.

About This Book

This book assumes that you have a Minecraft account and know the controls of the game. You're relatively familiar with how to destroy, craft, and place blocks — thus, this book focuses on explaining the skills that are necessary to manipulate blocks in interesting ways.

If you're new to Minecraft, this book can give you some ideas for getting started on your creative journey — and introduce you to the fundamental principles behind Minecraft construction. If you're already an experienced Minecrafter, though, you can use this book to gather some new perspectives on the subject or find inspiration if you feel like you've run out of things to build.

You'll never run out of things to build in Minecraft. Just look around for inspiration and you'll start thinking of new ideas in no time.

This book is updated to Version 1.8 of Minecraft. However, even when future versions of the game are released, the fundamental nature of Minecraft construction won't change much.

Foolish Assumptions

Throughout the course of this book, we assume the following things about you:

- You have a computer, and you know how to use it.
- You have a working copy of Minecraft, and you know how to move around the world.

Icons Used in This Book

This book contains some notable paragraphs that are marked with the following special icons:

This icon marks a tip that can help you improve your building skills.

This information is important to read, especially if you're just skimming the book. If you remember the information marked by these icons, you can improve your construction process to create bigger and better structures.

This icon appears rarely, but you should read it wherever it comes up. It warns you about pitfalls you should avoid when building so that you don't mess up your hard work.

Though the preceding icons indicate particularly important information, this one marks content you can easily skip, if you want. The icon refers to some of the technical details behind Minecraft construction, making it optional but interesting.

Conventions Used in This Book

In *Minecraft Construction For Dummies*, Portable Edition, we use numbered steps, bullet lists, and screen shots for your reference. we also provide a few sidebars containing information that isn't required reading but may help you understand a topic a little better. Web addresses appear in a special mono-type font that looks like this:

```
www.dummies.com
```

Where to Go From Here

If you have done little Minecraft construction in the past, the first few chapters are just right for you. The rest of the book is more topic-oriented, focusing on various aspects of construction that you may find helpful.

Occasionally, *For Dummies* technology books are updated. If this book has technical updates, they'll be posted at www.dummies.com/go/minecraftupdates.

1

Getting Started with Minecraft Construction

In This Chapter

▶ Coming up with ideas for buildings

▶ Stockpiling your building materials

▶ Managing your inventory

▶ Starting off the structure

*I*n Minecraft, you can build all kinds of different structures, and in many interesting environments. The basic concepts are simple (gather blocks and stack them), but you need a lot of practice in order to master the subject. In fact, when you first start out in Minecraft, you might find it difficult to develop a clear picture of exactly *what* you want to build, which materials you need, how big the building should be, and how you should go about constructing it. This chapter shows you how to build some basic sorts of creations, and how to get started with this essential feature of the game of Minecraft.

Evaluating Your Options

You can build lots of items using the blocks available to you in Minecraft. Here are just a few of the options:

✔ **Shacks and shelters:** Many players start out by building simple little huts for shelter during the (often dangerous) nights. See the following section for how to build these shelters quickly, efficiently, and easily.

- **Houses and mansions:** Many players tend to live in houses or even mansions. You can find lots of wooden, stone, and metal blocks in order to build these structures.

- **Castles:** Some players like to build huge castles out of stone, decorating them with carpets, tapestries, stained glass windows, and other luxuries.

- **Underground hideouts:** Some players abandon the surface world and build their homes in caves or other underground buildings.

- **Gardens:** Players who want a more natural creation can fill grassy areas with plant life and similar decorations. Chapter 10 describes how to build all sorts of different gardens.

- **Functional buildings:** Some buildings serve special purposes — you can make "automatic" farms that harvest themselves or have buildings that house machines capable of doing any number of things, like sort items or dispense potions, and other items to make your world look cool. See Chapter 12 in particular for details.

- **Villages and cities:** If you're feeling ambitious, you can build tons of different buildings and then connect them using roads or pathways.

- **Floating buildings:** Most blocks in Minecraft won't fall if there's nothing solid under them. (The only exceptions we can think of are sand, red sand, and gravel.) That means you can easily lift your structures high into the sky. It looks pretty neat — try it.

- **Artificial landscapes:** Just as Minecraft's world generator can create mountains, trees, and rivers, so can you. All you need are the right blocks and tools, and you can create items well beyond those that the game initially offers you — such as trees the size of skyscrapers. See Chapter 3 for more on this topic.

- **Bridges and roads:** These structures are, of course, good for traveling, but they're also useful for furnishing and connecting other buildings. Just think about the last time you walked from one building to another on a skybridge.

- **Miniature structures (statues and light posts, for example):** In Minecraft, blocks are very large — two of them stand taller than you (as a player, that is).

Designing *small* items in Minecraft can be a challenge, but it's fast and rewarding — and entirely possible with the right blocks.

 ✔ **Temples, parks, spires, and other aesthetic structures:** In Minecraft, you can build anything that exists in the real world — as well as many things that don't. If you have an idea of a structure or decoration you want to make, chances are you can do it in Minecraft.

With enough practice, you can design any of these sorts of buildings — and whatever else you can think of.

 Know what sorts of blocks are at your disposal. Play in Creative mode so that you can use every block — this strategy can help you understand which resources you can use in future projects. This also means you don't have to obtain every block in Survival mode, which can be rather time consuming.

Gathering Materials for Construction

Every building is composed of blocks, most of which are pulled straight from the inventory. The faster you can obtain and apply the inventory, the faster and easier you can design buildings.

Arranging the inventory in Creative mode

When building in Creative mode, you can add any item you want to the inventory. But it still helps a lot to know how you want the inventory organized. For example, you might store a few items that you tend to use a lot, and replace them whenever you need to.

Using the Creative Mode menu

To open your inventory menu, all you have to do is press the letter e on your keyboard — the default key, in other words. After opening the menu, note the 12 tabs — ten on the left and two on the right.

If you open the inventory menu in Creative mode, you'll see something quite different from Survival mode. Rather than show only the items in the inventory, the menu in Creative mode shows a huge list of almost every block and item in the game, which you can freely add to your inventory slots. Creative mode is a good thing: You can scroll through the blocks using either the scroll wheel or the slider on the right side of the menu.

If you don't want to spend a lot of time looking for the item you want, the menu is surrounded by 12 clickable tabs you can use to narrow your search and complete projects much faster. The most important tabs are described in this list:

✔ **Building Blocks:** The tab in the upper left corner, represented by the Bricks icon, contains most of the building blocks you use in your buildings. This section has over 150 blocks, though, so it can still be hard to find the blocks you need — the Search Items tab (explained later in this list) often works better.

✔ **Decoration Blocks:** This tab, represented by peonies (a type of flower), contains a lot of blocks that are usually used for detail and decorations, including functional blocks such as crafting tables and jukeboxes.

✔ **Redstone:** Represented by a lump of redstone dust, this tab has all the implements that affect — or can be affected by — redstone engineering. You generally don't need this section when doing construction work, unless you want to add circuitry to your building. (See Chapter 12 for more on this topic.) However, this section contains some commonly used blocks, such as doors and fence gates.

✔ **Transportation:** This small section, which is represented by a booster rail, has all the blocks having to do with assisted transportation (such as minecarts, boats, rails, saddles, and the beloved carrot on a stick).

✔ **Miscellaneous:** Represented by a lava bucket, this tab has a ton of miscellaneous items. Though most of them aren't useful for construction, a few items can be helpful — particularly the beacon, buckets of water or lava, and the various mob-summoning eggs.

✔ **Foodstuffs, Tools, Combat, Brewing, and Materials:** The five tabs at the lower left contain food items, tools, weapons, potions, and crafting materials. None of these is helpful for construction, so you only need to look at these tabs when you're setting up games or adventures for Survival mode players.

✔ **Search Items:** This section (not really a tab, we admit) is represented by the Compass icon — which actually works, even on the Inventory menu. This tab — probably the most useful tool in your possession — contains a text box you can type in. When you start typing the name of an item (or even just part of the name), the tab displays all items that have those same letters. For example, if you type lium in the box, the tab shows Allium and Mycelium. That makes it *easy* to find an item.

✔ **Survival Inventory:** Represented by a chest in the lower right corner of the Menu screen, this tab shows a screen that looks more like the Survival mode inventory. You can see all four rows of the inventory, a character portrait, and the slots where you can equip your armor. There's no place for crafting items, but you can do this with a crafting table. There's also an extra slot, labeled Destroy Item — you can either place items into this slot to delete them or shift+click the slot to clear the item in that spot.

If you hold down the Shift key before clicking on an item on the Creative mode menu, you get a full *stack* of those items — the largest number that can fit in a single inventory slot. For example, if you shift+click on a dirt block on this menu, you pick up 64 of those dirt blocks.

You can pick up an item, click on a different tab, and then place the item. You can then easily bring an item from the Creative mode menu into any slot of the inventory.

Applying the Pick Block key

Pick Block is an ability exclusive to Creative mode — you can use it to obtain any block in the inventory just by looking at the same type of block in the world.

By default, the Pick Block key is Button 3, or the middle mouse button — you can use it by pressing down on the scroll wheel. If your computer doesn't have a scroll wheel, go to the game's Options menu and reassign Pick Block to a different key (such as R or F, which you can use easily alongside the default controls).

Pick Block lets you do one of three things: Select a block in the inventory, put a selected block into the inventory, or delete and replace a block in the inventory. Here's how it works:

- ✏ If you have a certain kind of block in the bottom row of the inventory and you use Pick Block on the same type of block in the world, the block in the inventory is automatically selected.

- ✏ If you have an empty slot in the bottom row of the inventory and you use Pick Block on a block in the world, that block is put in the inventory.

- ✏ If you select a block in the inventory and use Pick Block on any type of block in the world, the originally selected block is deleted and replaced with the new block.

This feature is incredibly useful when building in Creative mode. You can use it in a few different ways, to

- ✏ **Fix or modify surfaces:** Suppose that you've accidentally broken part of a floor or that you want to add blocks to a landscape or surface. If you don't have the necessary block in the inventory but you're surrounded by the kind of block you need, you can just use Pick Block on the surface to obtain and use the same kind of block.

- ✏ **Manage the palette:** Using Pick Block is usually easier than trying to find the block you need in the inventory. Plus, if you replace a block in the inventory and realize that you need it again, there's a good chance that the block is nearby and you can use the Pick Block tool on it.

- ✏ **Copy structures:** If you want to build a structure that is similar to another, use Pick Block to copy some of the other structure's blocks into the inventory. This makes the building process much easier.

If you use the Pick Block feature on a mob instead of a block, you can obtain the corresponding egg for that mob. You can find these eggs on the Inventory menu in Creative mode and use them to summon mobs. This is useful when you want villagers, cattle, or other creatures in the structure.

You can also use the Pick Block feature on an item already in the inventory. You end up with a copy of the item on the cursor, and you can place it anywhere. If you use the Pick Block key on an item in the inventory that can be put into stacks (storing many of them in the same slot), you create a full stack of those items.

Obtaining a good inventory in Survival mode

It's harder to obtain tools in Survival mode than it is in Creative mode, mostly because of these issues:

✔ **You have to find all the items you need to use.** Unlike in Creative mode, there's no handy menu where you can go to get them.

✔ **Most items you use leave the inventory.** If you need more of something, you have to make or find more of it. When you use items like arrows or seeds or the like in Creative mode, they don't leave your inventory.

✔ **You can't break blocks instantly.** It's a bummer because some blocks take a long time to break, and they require tools if you want to break them quickly. And certain blocks (such as smooth stone) don't return the same item to the inventory when you destroy them.

✔ **You can't fly.** Unfortunately, flight is a luxury reserved for Creative mode. You have to get creative if you need to reach tall places.

What all this means is that in Survival mode you need to have a lot more items on hand than you do in Creative mode. For example, if you're going to use quite a bit of a particular block in a project, you should gather a lot of those blocks in the inventory before you start.

To give you an idea of what we're talking about, Figure 1-1 shows the inventory of a player who's about to start building.

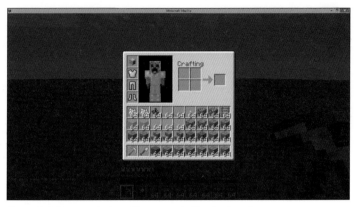

Figure 1-1: You need a lot of inventory in Survival mode.

For any large-scale building project, bring these items with you when you start:

- **Tools:** In case you need to destroy a block for whatever reason, bringing tools with you saves a few resources and a ton of time. The tools you bring depend on the sort of blocks you're working with:
  - *Pickaxes* help destroy stone- and metal-based blocks.
  - *Axes* are good at destroying wooden blocks.
  - *Shovels* are best against soft blocks such as dirt, sand, or gravel.

- **The main blocks you want to build with:** These can be just about anything, though most players have wooden planks, cobblestone, or the like.

- **Any decoration blocks that you want to place immediately:** You can place decorations as you build, but we suggest saving them until after you complete the general structure of the building.

- **Other necessary items:** For example, the inventory shown earlier, in Figure 1-1, includes bonemeal, which you need if you want to grow various plants (including saplings, which are also in the player's inventory).

Always gather more materials than you need. If you acquire too much, you can save the leftovers for future projects. If you acquire too little, you have to go all the way back in order to gather more.

In Survival mode or Creative mode, put your most commonly used items in the first four slots of the bottom row of the inventory. The keys to access these slots are much easier to reach, because the 1–4 keys are closer to the default movement keys. You can also use the scroll wheel to select different objects in your hot-bar, and it's easier to do that if similar items are grouped close together.

Creating Your First Building

After you have the necessary materials in the inventory, you can start practicing your construction tactics. The chapters later in this book offer a lot more advice on actual construction, but this section can help you get started.

Figure 1-2 shows how a player's construction ability might evolve over time. The building on the left is a shack built to store items and survive the night. The building in the middle is a detailed but fairly small house. Finally, the building on the right is an elegant mansion with a lot more detail than the other two structures.

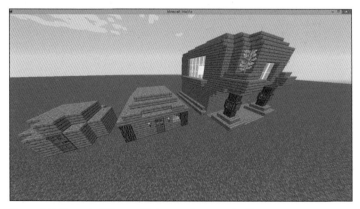

Figure 1-2: Three buildings with increasing complexity.

The general process behind creating a building is as follows:

1. **Decide where you want to build a building.**

   Any environment works fine, but you may have specific preferences, such as on a mountain or in a jungle.

2. **Decide on a texture for the building.**

   Do you want the building to be wooden? Or stone? Or metal? Or made of solid diamond? The texture of the building determines its theme, so think about it when planning out the architecture. This also helps you know which materials to gather.

3. **Plan out a single layer of the building.**

   In a traditional structure, it's the first floor. If you want the building to have interesting vertical structures (such as towers or stairwells), plan them out now.

4. **Construct all rooms and areas in that layer.**

   Do some interior decorating now if you want to see what your future masterpiece will look like.

5. **Keep constructing more layers until the building is complete.**

6. **Finish any details you want.**

   This step includes filling empty rooms and designing small decorations. Later chapters in this book give you tips on what to do and what not to do, but the best way to find out what you like and what works (or doesn't) is to practice. Design what you think is best, and don't be afraid to change your creation if you don't like something about it.

2

Building in Survival Mode

In This Chapter

- Managing your resources
- Getting from here to there on a building site
- Gathering resources

*W*hen you first log into Minecraft, you'll quickly find that there are two game modes you can explore, Survival mode and Creative mode. In Survival mode, you have to take the time to collect all of the resources you use and make use of tools to progress. However, in Creative mode, you can fly and break blocks instantly, as well as have access to an infinite amount of resources. Working in Survival mode is a lot different from working in Creative mode, and you need to keep track of, and watch out for, a few things when in that particular mode. In this chapter, we show you how to estimate and manage your resources as well as how to make your way around a building. We also talk about different ways to gather resources.

Keeping Track of your Resources

Figuring out how to keep track of your materials is one of the big challenges of Survival mode. You don't want to run out of resources in the middle of a project, and it's helpful to have your materials organized and easily accessible. This section can help you gather all the resources necessary to complete your build.

Estimating resources

Many structures require a lot of blocks, so you should err on the side of overestimating the resources you'll need for a build. If you end up with too many materials, you can simply store the extras in a chest somewhere — but if you don't have enough materials on hand, you have to put your project on hold while you go find more.

Our advice? Collect all your blocks ahead of time. You'll have a better idea of the materials you have (or don't have), and you'll be more organized when you start building.

Different types of structures require different amounts of blocks. For example, detailed builds often have at least 1,000 blocks, and large builds can easily have over 10,000 blocks.

For that number of blocks, you need a lot of stacks. A *stack* of items is equal to a single inventory slot. In other words, when you open your inventory by pressing (the default) e button on your keyboard, you'll see your 36 inventory slots. Each inventory slot holds up to 64 blocks (which isn't really that much when you need 1,000 or more blocks).

This list of build types gives you examples to help you estimate the resources you need for a project:

- ✔ **A temporary build** might be a storage room to store items safely or a shack you'd use as a hiding place from mobs. These builds are usually built as a 6x6x6 cube and take only 150 blocks (and sometimes fewer).

- ✔ **A tiny build** might be a small house that has one or two rooms. You can build it as a 12x12x12 cube. A structure such as this should take between 300 and 600 blocks.

- ✔ **A small build** can start taking up some serious space. Small structures can hold most items you need, and you can make them more than one story tall. A small build would be something like a 20x20x20 cube, which would take between 800 and 4,000 blocks, depending on how tightly packed it is. (Think a two story house, or a restaurant.)

✔ **A medium build** is what most projects are. They could be something along the lines of a manor or a market-place. Often times they vary in size and can take quite a while to build. A medium build could be a 50x50x50 cube and usually takes between 5,000 and 50,000 blocks.

✔ **A large build** is about the size of a three-story mansion. It could be up to a 100x100x100 cube and could take any-where from 4 million to 7.5 million blocks to build. You definitely need to plan on spending a lot of time building one of these.

✔ **A huge build** is a castle or giant monument that can really only fit in a 500x100x500 space. It takes from 40 million to 62.5 million blocks to build.

✔ **An epic build,** the largest type of build, is usually done with a big group of people — and even then it can still take a truly long time to create. Epic builds, which include cities and enormous castles, can cover any size you want.

For the average build, you need about 15 to 150 stacks of the materials you want to use depending on big the build is. Based on this number and the guidelines in this list, you should be able to estimate how many blocks you need for your build.

Organizing your materials

When you start a build, it's a good idea to gather all your materials in one place. Going back and forth between gather-ing, crafting, and building is a pain. It's a lot easier if every-thing is in the same place before you start. To organize your materials, follow these steps:

1. **Figure out what you need.**

   Decide what kinds of blocks you want to include in your build, and make sure that you know how to get them.

2. **Set up chests and crafting stations.**

   Before you start on a project, it's a good idea to set up a few chests and crafting tables. This will make it so that a) you don't have to run back and forth to get items and b) you have quick access to things like furnaces. If you need to store items you're going to need for a build, or if you decide you want to put a project on hold, you're going to need a place to store your materials safely. Also, bringing various crafting tables along with you means you don't have to run between your build site and your base all the time. Crafting tables are useful for making slabs and stairs on the go, and ender chests let you access your best equipment immediately. It's also nice to have a furnace nearby for cooking. Figure 2-1 shows a simple building setup with chests and crafting tables you can put together before you start building.

3. **Gather all the raw materials you need.**

   You should have a handy list ready if you did Step 1. Most buildings require lots of wooden planks or cobblestone. If your inventory fills up, place the materials into some of the chests. (If you're only working on a small project, you probably don't have to worry about this step.)

4. **Craft all the other materials you need.**

   Make fences, stairs, and everything else you need. For these types of items — the ones you craft yourself — don't go overboard; only make the bare minimum. If you run out of crafted materials, you can always craft more.

5. **Sort your resources.**

   Put your resources in your inventory and organize them so that you can easily find everything when you need it. Sort into chests any items you can't hold.

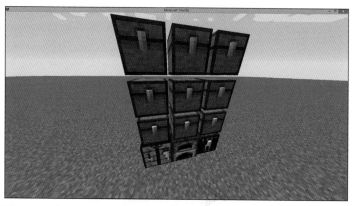

Figure 2-1: Construction resources.

Getting around the Structure

In Creative mode, you can fly and move quickly around buildings — in Survival mode, you can't, meaning you have to come up with ways to move around. In Survival mode, you sometimes have to get creative with how you navigate the build. The following sections show you tricks to help you with this task.

Using scaffolding

If you need to build in hard-to-reach areas, you can use *scaffolding*. In other words, you can build a pillar of blocks as high as you need so that you can build items such as roofs and tall towers. To use scaffolding, follow these steps:

1. **Get some easy-to-break blocks, like dirt or sand blocks.**

   Dirt or sand blocks are best for temporary structures because you can place them and destroy them pretty easily. If you're wealthy in your Minecraft world and can afford lots of diamond tools, you can use blocks like wood or cobblestone instead.

2. Using the mouse, "look" straight down while standing next to the place you want to climb up to.

3. Hold down the Use Item button (or just right-click, by default), jump, and place one of your blocks under you.

   You're building a pillar that raises you up so that you can work.

4. Continue looking down and repeating Step 3 until you're as high as you need to be to work.

5. To then place blocks horizontally at your new level, press the Shift key so you can crawl to the very edge of the blocks, then place the block there.

6. Continue placing blocks horizontally until you've reached where you need to be to continue building.

7. When you're done with your work, stand on the pillar of blocks you've built, look down, and hold the Attack button.

   You're destroying all the blocks in the pillar so that you can get down to the ground.

Figure 2-2 shows you what scaffolding might look like.

Figure 2-2: A scaffold made of dirt.

Sand and gravel make good scaffolding because they're easy to destroy. If you destroy the bottom block of a sand or gravel pillar and then quickly replace it with a torch or another non-solid block, the pillar collapses into a pile of sand or gravel items for you.

Using ladders to scale your structure

Ladders are cheap, and they help you climb walls quickly. They are also incredibly versatile and can get you out of a lot of situations. We show you how to build a ladder in Chapter 4 but now we want to show you how to scale a wall with ladders. Just follow these steps:

1. **Walk up to the wall and put the ladder in your hot bar either by pressing the corresponding number or by navigating to it with the scroll wheel.**

2. **Press and hold the Use Item button (right-click, by default).**

3. **Keep your eye on the wall and hold the Forward key (W, by default) to climb the ladder.**

   As you climb, you can place more ladders in front of you by holding down the Use Item button.

Teleporting with Ender pearls

Ender pearls, which you get from killing endermen, make for an easy way to get around your building. You can throw ender pearls a long way, and you'll teleport to wherever they land. With good aim, you can move around pretty easily.

Powering up with potions

You can also use potions to help you get around your building. The most popular potions are speed (to run faster), night vision (to see better in dark areas), and water breathing (to stay underwater). The water breathing potion lets you stay underwater only until the potion wears off, which, depending on how you brew it, could be from three minutes to eight minutes. (Note that the water breathing potion grants you improved vision underwater as well.)

To create these potions, follow these instructions:

1. **Craft some glass bottles.**

   You can make glass bottles with 3 glass blocks.

2. **Fill the bottles with water.**

   Click the Use Item button (right-click by default) while holding your glass bottles and looking at a body of water.

3. **Place the bottles of water in a brewing stand, and add a nether wart.**

   To get a brewing stand, you need to set three smooth-stone and one blaze rod in an upside-down "T" design. You can get nether wart in nether fortresses; it can also be grown on soulsand.

   This converts the water into Awkward Potions.

4. **Use the brewing stand again to add the final ingredient you need to complete a particular potion.**

   Use sugar for speed, a golden carrot for night vision, and a pufferfish for water breathing.

Speeding up construction with beacons

Of all the options for moving around a build, the beacon is the most expensive — but it's also a valuable resource to have. Beacons constantly "buff up" any player within a certain radius. (More on that in a bit.)

To use a beacon, you have to place it on a pyramid made of iron, gold, diamond, or emerald blocks. The larger the pyramid, the greater the area it affects (but pyramids can only be 4 layers or fewer). Figure 2-3 shows what a high-level beacon looks like.

Figure 2-3: An active beacon.

Beacons provide several different status effects, such as haste, regeneration, and jump boost. When you're near the beacon, you can use any of those effects to work on your build much faster.

An active beacon fires a beam of light into the sky — it won't activate if there's a solid block above it. However, it's fine to place transparent blocks like glass over a beacon and if you use stained glass it will color the beacon's light.

Collecting Resources

You can collect resources in several ways — some are more efficient than others. This section shows you different ways to gather materials for your structure.

You have a couple of different options when it comes to mining. Each one has its pros and cons, so it's up to you to decide which one you want to use.

Quarrying

Quarrying is the easiest way to mine — you just dig a huge hole in the ground and keep digging it as deep as it will go. Mining out a quarry can take a while because you're mining a lot of blocks at one time. The good thing about quarries is that they grab every single resource from the patch of land you're digging out. You don't get as many valuable ores, but you gain tons of cobblestone and a nice spot for a future underground structure.

In the example shown in Figure 2-4, every time the player dug out a layer of stone, he placed the next piece in a large stairwell so that he could get out of the quarry. You can do this too, with blocks, stairs, ladders, and so on.

Figure 2-4: A quarry with a stairwell.

Strip mining

Strip mining gets you a good amount of cobblestone and some valuable minerals. To start strip mining, follow these steps:

1. **Dig deep underground.**

   If you stay about 13 blocks above the bottom of the world — meaning if you press f3, your Y coordinate should read 13 — you can get the most valuable ores.

2. **Dig straight in any direction.**

   Place torches along the way so that you don't get attacked by hostile mobs on your way back.

3. **If a ravine or lava gets in your way, or you just don't feel like going in a straight line anymore, move 3 blocks to the side and build a parallel tunnel.**

   Your tunnels are separated by a gap that's 2 blocks wide. This arrangement ensures that you can see any valuable minerals you come across without having to spend tons of time mining.

   Figure 2-5 diagrams the top view of an organized strip mine.

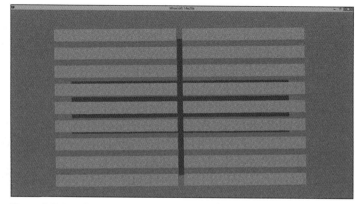

Figure 2-5: A typical strip mine.

Cave mining

Cave mining is useful for getting valuable ores, but not so useful if you're trying to get cobblestone. To start cave mining, find a big cave, explore it, and mine out all resources you see along the way. Be careful, though: You'll probably run into enemies when you're exploring dark caves. Make sure that you have a way to defend yourself.

When your cave is tapped out, you can switch to one of the other mining options.

Build a beacon with the Haste power-up to mine faster and get tons of stone and minerals.

3

Setting Up Your Building Site

*B*efore you start building, you need to figure out where to build. Plains and deserts generally make for usable, flat building ground, but what if you want to build your structure on a mountain? Or what if you can't find a flat area that's large enough to build a mansion?

This chapter explains the two ways of solving topographical issues: Adapt to the landscape, and make the landscape adapt to you. In Minecraft, almost everything is changeable — you can use that knowledge to your advantage.

Building on Interesting Landscapes

A building doesn't have to stand on its own — lots of interesting structures build from their surroundings. For example, you can build a fortress inside a cave, a city around a mountain, or a swamp town connected by bridges. Plus, using your surroundings as part of your building can save you a ton of building time because you're taking advantage of the thousands of blocks that have already been placed for you.

For example, Figure 3-1 shows a bunch of little houses built in an Extreme Hills biome with ladders and stairwells connecting them. This unusual arrangement looks like something out of a fantasy book — and the building process was definitely easier than building a structure of our own and planting houses in it.

Figure 3-1: A mountain town.

If you want to create a building on an existing natural structure, follow these steps:

1. **Decide how much of the building can fit inside the natural structure.**

   If you want to build on a mountain, see how much you can put in or around the mountain without extending too far out (you don't want your structure to look imbalanced). Or, if you want to build in a cave, decide how much of the structure should fit inside the cave. Remember that the structure isn't limited to these boundaries — you're simply deciding where to start. You can change things later.

2. **Dig out the landscape to make way for your buildings.**

   If your mountain or forest or another structure begins to look too porous, stop digging for now — your creation may end up blotting out the landscape rather than working with it.

3. **Construct any large buildings that tie together the theme of the structure.**

   This includes giant bridges, large buildings, and transportation systems that go throughout the natural structures.

4. **Create the rest of your buildings.**

   While you work, step back every once in a while to make sure that the buildings still fit in with the landscape.

5. **Decorate the interiors of your buildings.**

   After the outside looks good, all you have to do is finish up the details.

Every biome supports different building styles — a desert may lend itself to a temple, for example, or a Jungle biome may be a good location for a tree house. Work wherever you like.

Reshaping the Landscape

Though landscapes allow for lots of neat-looking creations, sometimes the landscape you have isn't quite the one you want. Fortunately, you can change the world however you want — it just takes some time.

A common problem when building is finding level ground to build on. Even plains aren't completely level, which makes it tricky to build structures with flat floors. Fortunately, you can rebuild your surroundings in many ways, as described in the following two sections.

Leveling mostly flat surfaces

If a surface has a few bumps and dips, you can make it completely flat by following these steps:

1. **Get the largest piece of flat land you can find.**

   Look for a lot of blocks that are all at the same elevation.

2. **Destroy any small hills inside the land.**

   Make sure it has no blocks taller than the stretch of land.

3. **Fill any holes in the land.**

   You can use any block you want for this step, including dirt or sand. And you don't necessarily have to fill the holes entirely — you can probably get away with just covering the top of the hole.

   Some issues might arise from covering just the top of any holes. These hollow spaces might create spawning spaces that slow down mob spawning, and they could make it harder to terraform the land later. In other words, it's probably in your best interest to fill up holes completely rather than just covering them in a layer of dirt, but we leave that up to you.

4. **Level other hills and holes at the edge of the land, extending the land until it's big enough to support your building.**

Leveling large structures

Sometimes you want even more room to build a structure. You might destroy an entire hill to make way for your building, for example, or hollow out a mountain to build an underground home.

Some players dig out these structures by hand — beacons and enchantments give you Haste and Efficiency power-ups so that you can mine out an area quickly. However, if you have a plentiful source of sand and gunpowder, you can use another method to clear out land: TNT.

To mine out a large areas with TNT, you can follow one of two different methods:

✔ **Maintain a distance of at least 3 to 5 blocks between each block of TNT you use.** This method is the safer one. When you spread out explosives this way, you can carve out holes in any shape you want, hollowing out caves or reducing hills to flatter surfaces.

✔ **Place a cluster of TNT (for example, a 3x3x3 cube) at the center of the place you want to destroy.** This method is riskier and inaccurate — but it's easier to complete.

When TNT is in close quarters like this, some of the explosives tend to launch off-course and can destroy other structures (even those you want to keep).

You can light TNT in lots of simple ways after you place it. You can use pressure plates, redstone torches, flint and steel, bows with the Flame enchantment, and many other tools. None of these methods changes the way the TNT detonates, so use whichever one is most convenient.

Editing the Landscape with Commands

When you play in Creative mode, you can create structures much faster than you can in Survival mode, and you can more easily manipulate the natural landscape.

Worlds in Creative mode allow for *cheat commands* by default. You enter these strings of text into the Chat menu — just press the "T" key to open the menu, then type in the command you need to create various effects. These commands can summon and teleport entities, produce items, massively edit the world, and perform tons of other tasks if you know how to use them.

For example, Figure 3-2 shows gigantic stretches of flat land that were created in seconds by using commands.

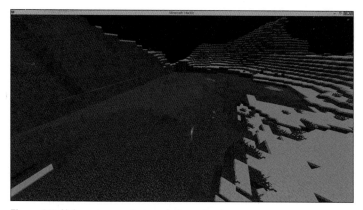

Figure 3-2: Using commands to redefine a landscape.

You can execute commands in other ways, but for the construction-based commands covered in this book, stick to the Chat menu.

In Minecraft, a *command* consists of a set of words or numbers separated by spaces. The first word defines the command being cast, and the following words all define the command's *arguments* (the various terms and variables that determine exactly how the command works).

To enter a command into the Chat menu, first type a slash (/) and then the commands you want to use.

A few commands let you modify the world as fast as you possibly can. The following sections show you how to use some of these commands to make your Minecraft experience easier.

Filling areas with the Fill command

One of the most commonly used construction commands is /fill. You can use this command to place lots of blocks in a certain area instantly. To use this command, follow these steps:

1. **Go to a corner of the area you want to fill.**

   The Fill command affects blocks in a box-shaped region, up to 32,768 blocks in volume. Pick any of the 8 corners of the box you want to fill.

2. **Press F3 (⌘ F3 on a Mac).**

   This step displays a bunch of information about the current game.

3. **Record your coordinates.**

   Part of the information displayed in F3 mode is a line that says Block: followed by three numbers. These numbers tell you where exactly your character is. The X and Z coordinates of your character tell you where you are on the plane parallel to the ground, whereas your Y coordinate tells you your height. Make a note of these numbers because you'll need to write them into the command later.

4. **Move to the opposite corner of the area you want to fill.**

5. **Record the coordinates there.**

   Alternatively, use relative coordinates: A tilde (~) in a command indicates that a coordinate is relative to your own position. So ~ ~ ~ indicates your current position, and ~ ~-1 ~ indicates the block below you.

6. **Press the "T" key to open the Chat menu and type /** fill [*your first coordinates*] [*your second coordinates*].

   For example, you might enter /fill 1123 20 16 1122 30 -16.

7. **Enter a space, and then type** minecraft: **(or press Tab as a shortcut).**

   Every block in this game has a technical name, such as minecraft:stone, minecraft:planks, or minecraft:redstone_torch. The first part is necessary only for autocompletion purposes, as described in Step 8. If you already know the technical name of the block, don't type only **minecraft:**; go ahead and type **minecraft:stone** or **minecraft:planks** or whatever the name is, and then skip to Step 10. If you don't know the technical name of the block, stick with Step 7 as written and then go on to Step 8.

8. **Press Tab to see a list of block names.**

   From here, you can find the block that you want to fill the area. If you know that its name starts with a certain couple of letters, type those letters, and then press Tab for a narrower search. After you see which block you want to use type it after the **minecraft:**.

9. **Press the spacebar again and enter the data value of the block.**

   This is 0 by default — if you select another number, it chooses a variant of the block. For example, wooden planks have a different color based on the data value you give them.

   Steps 9 and 10 are optional — however, if you complete Step 10, you *must* complete this one as well.

10. **Press the spacebar again, and enter a keyword indicating how to handle blocks that are already inside the fill area.**

    You can pick one of five different keywords:

    - *replace:* With this keyword, when you fill the target area, any block already in that area is replaced. Alternatively, you can type **replace** followed by a space and then the name of another block (see Steps 7 and 8). This makes it so that the /fill command replaces every block of that type only in the target area rather than filling up the whole area. (Note that replace is the default keyword.) At this point the command should look like /fill 1123 20 16 1122 30 -16 minecraft:wool 1 replace.

    - *destroy:* All existing blocks in the target area are destroyed, just as though a player mined them.

    - *keep:* This command does not affect blocks already in the target area (except for air, of course).

    - *hollow:* With this command, only the outer layer of the target area is filled with blocks — all blocks on the inside are replaced with air.

    - *outline:* Only the outer layer of the target area is filled with blocks, but blocks on the inside remain as they were.

Don't be put off by the length of these instructions — the more you practice, the easier (and faster) it is.

The process in the preceding step list works best when you don't quite know the size of the area you want to fill. But if you want to fill an area that you know is 10x10x20, for example, there's a faster way to do it:

1. **Go to a corner of the area you want to fill.**

   This part is just like the other method, but it's done for a different purpose.

2. **Press F3.**

   In addition to pulling up a menu, the F3 button changes the crosshair in the center of the screen into a symbol composed of a red segment, a green segment, and a blue segment where green is the Y direction, red is the X direction, and blue is the Z direction. These segments point in the positive x-direction, y-direction, and z-direction, respectively. (For example, if you move along the red line, the x-coordinate should increase.)

3. **Use the crosshair to figure out the relative coordinates of the opposite corner.**

   For example, if the crosshair numbers read ~100 ~-5 ~2, the opposite corner is 100 blocks in the X-direction, -5 blocks in the Y-direction, and 2 blocks in the Z-direction.

4. **Open the chat menu and type** /fill ~ ~ ~ [relative coordinates].

   For example, to create a platform 100 blocks long and 100 blocks wide, where one corner is where you are and the opposite corner is at 99 ~ ~99, type /fill ~ ~ ~ ~99 ~ ~99.

5. **Complete the process as per usual (see Steps 7–10 in the preceding step list).**

Copying structures with the Clone command

The helpful /clone command copies the blocks in a certain area and places them in another area. This is extremely useful for duplicating houses, towers, and other structures you want to build a lot of quickly. To clone a structure, follow these steps:

1. **Build the structure you want to clone (you can build it anywhere).**

2. **Determine the area you want to clone.**

   Imagine this area as an invisible box enclosing the structure. As with the /fill command, this box can't contain more than 32,768 blocks, so you may have to clone large structures piece by piece.

3. **Find the coordinates of two opposite corners of the invisible box.**

   This step is done just like it is with the /fill command (see the steps in the preceding section).

4. **Find the coordinates of the spot where you want to place the cloned structure.**

   You should have a total of three sets of coordinates recorded.

5. **Open the Chat menu and type** clone [first coordinates] [second coordinates] [destination coordinates].

   For example, you might type clone 302 3 2 300 1 0 ~ ~2 ~.

   Make sure your character is at least somewhat close to both the target that you're cloning and the destination where you're cloning it to. Minecraft can load only part of the world at a time. If the Clone command tries to access blocks that are too far away to be loaded, the command doesn't work and you see the error message Cannot access blocks outside of the world.

6. **Press the spacebar and enter a keyword stating how you want to execute the Clone command.**

   The /clone command has these three options:

   - *replace:* The target structure is cloned and replaces any blocks that are already in the target area. (Note that replace is the default option, so it's already entered; you don't have to be explicitly type it in.)

   - *masked:* Only non-air blocks are cloned — for example, you can potentially clone a hollow object so that it surrounds another object.

   - *filtered:* If you select this option, you *must* specify which blocks are not filtered. The idea here is that, after you write the command, you add a list of blocks separated by spaces (see the step list in the "Filling areas with the Fill command" section, earlier in this chapter, for tracking down the technical names of blocks.) When the command is executed, only blocks of the listed type are cloned.

7. **(Optional) Press the spacebar again, and enter another keyword explaining how the command works.**

   Again, you have three options:

   - *normal:* This is the default and thus does not need to be typed. You need to enter this keyword only if you selected the Filtered option in Step 6.

   - *move:* Every block that is cloned is replaced with air, so the structure is moved rather than cloned.

   - *force:* If this setting is active, the cloning process succeeds even if the destination area overlaps with the area being cloned. (This option normally results in an error message.)

Carving Out Land with Explosive Commands

Commands can also produce some interesting destructive effects if you use them correctly. You can carve holes or flats in many ways so that you can build on them (including using the /fill command in the previous section to replace large sections of land with air). However, if you want natural-looking negative space in the most efficient way possible, try out the destructive commands in this section.

A couple of basic commands are particularly useful:

```
/summon PrimedTnt
/summon EnderCrystal
```

The first command creates an instant explosion wherever your character is — all you have to do is approach an area and execute the command to produce an instant crater. The second command creates an ender crystal, which is a powerful explosive that is set off by any sort of damage. If you place these crystals sparsely throughout an area and then punch one of them, you can set off a devastating but controlled chain reaction.

Try putting the command /execute @p ~ ~ ~ summon PrimedTnt into a command block, a block that can have commands edited into it and, when powered with redstone, executes the entire command. Note that you can only get these blocks if you use *your username* command_block. Attaching it to a redstone loop (a device that constantly transmits power back and forth) creates a constant explosive force around you that lets you level out landscapes by simply moving through them.

Building Your Own, Natural Elements

Just as you can destroy mountains, trees, rivers, and other natural structures, you can also create them. This can be useful when you want to

- ✔ **Make your buildings look more natural.**
- ✔ **Blend your structures with the world around them.**
- ✔ **Make your environment more interesting.**

For example, Figure 3-3 shows a river and a few trees. These elements weren't created by the world generator; they were created by a player. You can definitely do this in Survival mode, and you can make useful additions to your world.

Figure 3-3: A custom river and trees.

You can design lots of natural elements — here are a few examples:

- ✔ **Hills and mountains:** These aren't quite as resource-intensive as they might seem. In fact, if you never plan to build *inside* the new hill or mountain, there's no need for there to *be* an inside. In a grassy biome, all you have to do is construct a hollow mound of dirt and wait for the grass to spread on top of it.

- ✔ **Trees:** Trees are constructed out of wood blocks and leaf blocks. Construct the wooden part first (to cement the tree's structure). Then gather some leaf blocks (you can't do this by hand — leaf blocks drop only if you use the Shears tool), and fill up the branches of the tree with them. Don't worry about the leaves decaying like they do in naturally generated trees — if you placed the leaf blocks, they don't go away unless you break them manually.

- ✔ **Rivers:** After you dig a canal, the tricky part about creating a river is filling the trench with water. Unlike in real life, you can't do this by simply pouring water into one side and waiting for it to fill up — see Chapter 9 for a closer look at how Minecraft handles water. The most direct way is to use buckets of water throughout the river until the whole thing is filled with water (you can even build waterfalls, just by letting the water flow over a ledge). However, if you have a lot of resources, you could enchant a tool with silk touch and gather ice instead — it's much easier to place ice blocks throughout the trench and then destroy them to turn them into water blocks.

4

Exploring Different Types of Builds

In This Chapter

▶ Doing your building prep work

▶ Constructing (and decorating) various buildings

▶ Creating cites

▶ Excavating underground

*I*n Minecraft, you can build any kind of structure you want — if you can imagine it, you can build it. And if you want, you can pack all those buildings into a small area and create a city. What's more, you can link those city buildings together with the help of underground passageways — some of them secret, some of them known to all.

So, if you're at all interested in erecting a building, creating a city, digging a tunnel, finding out how to mine, or making a secret passageway and room, you're in the right place! If you choose to read this entire chapter, you'll be able to do all these things.

Planning Buildings

We weren't kidding when we said you can build pretty much anything you can think of. Castles and basic houses are popular, but you can even build an igloo or a bunker.

Before you get started, you need to know that every kind of structure is called a *build*. You see that term a lot in this book. A build can be anything — a house, a shop, a tunnel, or even an entire city. The general term *build* refers to the process of building something.

Deciding what and where to build

Though you can simply dive in and start building, you should try to take some time to plan. We've found that planning saves a lot of time later. If you have random buildings scattered around, it's hard to fit new items in when you need them.

We start our planning process by choosing where and what to build, determining whether the building has a purpose, deciding on its size, and choosing items to put inside.

What's the most important part of real estate? Location! Location! Location! Where you build the new structure can affect how you design it. Ask yourself these questions: What biome will serve as your building's home? Will you build close to other buildings or in an isolated area? In a modern city or a small village? How does your build fit with nearby structures? For example, if you're building in a city, you may have to plan for a taller building that fits between others rather than a sprawling shopping mall.

Does the new structure have a purpose? Not every building does. Some are merely for decoration — just a way to make your city or village appear attractive and inviting. If that's the case, be sure to make the new building pretty, but invest more effort into the exterior decorations. (Most buildings that are used for decoration don't even have an inside.)

However, many buildings do have a purpose — especially in a city. Ask yourself these questions: How will you use the building? Do you need anything inside or outside the building in order to use it the way you want?

If your building has a specific purpose, compare it to buildings in real life. For example, you may have decided that your city needs a library (a place where people can either sit and read or check out books for home use). Out in the real world, any building that wants to act as a library has to have shelving, books, tables, chairs, and a circulation desk. You should plan on having those items in the library as well. Or, if you want to build a shop, think about what most shops have — display cases, for example, or perhaps changing rooms, shelving, and a checkout counter.

While it's good to have a building that resembles another in real life, you don't have to make it that way. It's your building, after all, so if you feel like it does or doesn't need something that the building has in real life, that's okay! Don't be afraid to make the building your own.

Estimating your building materials

To estimate the amount of materials you need, start out by making a wireframe of what you plan to build. Use the number of blocks you think you'll need for your actual building — the wireframe helps you see if you need more (or fewer) blocks. (See Chapter 5 for more about wireframes). This strategy helps you spot any flaws in your plan that you didn't notice earlier. You can also decide whether the building needs to be larger or smaller.

Now that you have an idea of what to build, how big the buildings should be, and where to build them, make a list of all the materials you need. For example, you need enough blocks to make the building the right size; for comparison's sake, a single-story, 2-room house requires at least 120 blocks.

There's more to a building than its walls and ceilings. You have to take into account the materials for windows (see Chapter 11) and plan for some decorations or machines (such as a stove). Flip over to Chapter 6 to see how to make machines.

Starting the Build

Time to break out the hard hats! This section explains how to build the building, step by step.

You can make a practice building, called a wireframe, so that you can try out different designs and shapes before you start building. See Chapter 5 to find out how to make a wireframe.

To keep things relatively easy, the instructions we came up with in the following section tell you how to build a basic house. Our reasoning here is that you can pretty much build any other building — large or small — when you know how to build a basic house. A house is a good starter project because everyone needs one. It's your home base, somewhere to sleep at night, and a place to switch out your tools.

A basic house uses wooden planks as walls and has two windows and a door. Any blocks can be used instead of wooden planks, but wooden planks are the easiest to acquire. You start by building the walls, and then the ceiling, and then the door.

Building walls

Walls provide stability for your house and a place to put the roof. They can also divide the interior space into separate rooms — just like they do in your real-life house. Follow these instructions to make walls:

1. Gather wood from trees.

You can get wood from trees by breaking their trunks. To break their trunks, right-click and hold until the trunk breaks. Be sure to gather as much wood as you think you will need.

If you want to speed up the process, you can make an axe. You don't necessarily need any tools to do this, but you need 3 cobblestone and 2 sticks. Place the first cobblestone in the upper left corner of your crafting table; the second cobblestone, in the middle box of the left column; and the last one, in the top box of the middle column. Next, place the 2 sticks in the remaining boxes of the middle row. The crafting table does its magic by exchanging everything you've added for an axe. (For more on how the crafting table works, see Chapter 1.)

2. **Place the wood in the crafting table.**

   There's no need to place them in a specific box — you can put them anywhere on the table. The crafting table exchanges them for wooden planks — one wood makes four wooden planks.

3. **Use the wooden planks to make the outline of your house.**

   This outline is the item we've referred to as a wire-frame. Figure 4-1 shows an example of a wireframe outline. For more information about wireframes, look at Chapter 5.

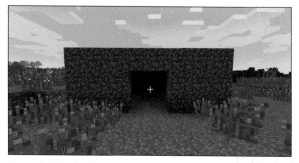

Figure 4-1: A wireframe outline for a basic house.

4. **Stack blocks on top of the wireframe, until the wall is finished.**

   Take a look at Figure 4-2 to see what we mean.

   The wall can be as tall as you want it to be, but remember that this is a simple house, so its walls shouldn't be over 5 blocks tall.

5. **Continue building walls until you have made all four.**

   All four walls should be the same height.

Figure 4-2: Making walls for a basic house.

Building a ceiling

After building all the walls, you still need something to keep
the rain out — a ceiling, in other words. To build the ceiling,
you use the same kind of wooden planks you used for the
walls. That way, you can match the walls' color and texture.

Ceilings should be around three blocks high — you need to
move around without hitting your head! — but that means
you need a way to reach higher. Here's how to do that:

1. **Place 1 block in front of you and jump on it.**

   To jump, just press the spacebar.

2. **Jump again and right-click to place another block
   under yourself.**

   The idea here is to create a sturdy platform that you
   can use to reach the top of the walls.

3. **Keep doing this until you're able to reach the top of
   the wall.**

4. **When you've reached the top of the wall, build from
   one wall to the opposite wall by placing blocks on
   the side of the blocks that make up the wall.**

   Figure 4-3 can help you see whether you're doing the
   right thing.

Figure 4-3: Creating a ceiling for a basic house.

Building a door

With the ceiling and walls in place, it's time to build a door to your house. To make a door, create a door frame by breaking 2 blocks in the wall. (One block should be on top of another.)

You can break a block at any time by left-clicking the block.

To make a door to fill the frame you created, you need six wooden planks. Place the wooden planks on the crafting table, filling the left and middle columns. Take the door in exchange for the planks. Then just right-click to place the door in the hole you made and you're done!

Brightening things up

Now that you have a safe place to rest at night, it's time to light it up. A torch is the most common way to light a room, and it's also the easiest to make. To make a torch, follow these simple steps:

1. **Gather one wood.**

   You get wood from trees by breaking their trunks. To break a trunk, right-click and hold until it breaks.

2. **Place the wood into crafting table (any box is fine) to turn it into 4 wooden planks.**

3. **Keep the planks in your inventory.**

4. **Place two of the planks on the crafting table, with one in the center box and another in the box below it.**

   The planks turn into sticks.

5. **Keep the sticks in the inventory.**

6. **Mine 1 coal using a pickaxe.**

   You can find more information about mining and pickaxes in the "Tunnel mining" section, later in this chapter.

   You can also use charcoal instead of coal. You can make charcoal by smelting wood in a furnace.

7. **Place the coal in the center box of the crafting table, and place a stick in the lower box of the middle row.**

8. **Take the lit torch that appears.**

You can place the torch anywhere in your house.

Another effective light source is the window. Windows provide natural light and make your house look brighter. To make windows, you need sand, a furnace, and some coal or charcoal (either one works). To get sand, find a beach and break sand blocks (left-click and hold until the block breaks) and pick up the sand.

To make a furnace, you need 8 cobblestones. Place the cobblestone on the crafting table, filling all the boxes except for the center box, and then take the furnace that appears. Now you use that furnace to make glass.

To use the furnace, right-click on it. Place the sand in the top box of the furnace, and place the coal in the bottom box. Wait until glass appears in the far right box, and take it.

Now you have glass, but you need a place to put it. To make a hole for the window, break a block of the wall at eye level. Place the glass block in that hole. Now you have a window in your house! For more information on windows, flip over to Chapter 11.

Adding more levels

So far, your house has only one level. If you want more space, simply make another level. To get started, you need to climb to the top of your building. Here's how to climb up and start the new level:

1. **Go outside to the side of your house, place 1 block in front of you, and jump on it.**

2. **Jump again and quickly place another block under yourself as you're in the air.**

3. **Do this until you reach the top of your house.**

4. **Build walls around you, as you did earlier in this chapter.**

   For an example, look at Figure 4-4.

   You can also use ladders to get to the top of your wall. Ladders are easy to make, but require more resources than the method above:

   To make a ladder, you need seven sticks. To make sticks, place two wooden planks into your crafting table, with one filling the box above the other. Two wooden planks will make four sticks, so do this twice.

Figure 4-4: Building the second floor of your house.

Now that you have the sticks you need, you can make a ladder. Place the first three sticks in the left column — one in each box. Place the next three sticks in the right column, also filling all the boxes in that column. Finally, place the last stick in the table's center box. If you have one stick left over, don't worry, you're supposed to. Take the 3 ladders you get for the sticks and you're done!

5. **Build a new ceiling above you, as you also did earlier.**

Now that you have a two-story house, add some of the elements we've described, such as windows and doors. You also need a way to move from one floor to the other. You don't have to make anything fancy — you can just make a hole in the floor of the top floor and leap down to the first level. Or you can build a stairway with blocks. For an example, look at Figure 4-5. The "Secret Rooms" section, later in this chapter gives you more information on stairs.

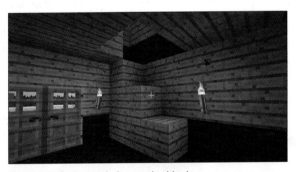

Figure 4-5: Stairs made by regular blocks.

You have completed your first building! If you think that the building is somewhat dull, don't be afraid to add some color to it. Play with different colors and types of blocks. For example, if you made a library, add bookshelves to the outside walls as decoration.

Building a City

Generally speaking, a *city* is a collection of buildings, roads, paths, and tunnels. Now, not all cities have all these elements, but these items truly help a city become more complete.

Most players build cities in Minecraft because it's fun and it's a nice challenge. Cities can have a lot of different buildings in them, and which buildings get built usually depends on the theme of the city. For example, a city can be Viking related, a village, or modern. Minecraft has hundreds of other themes too, so if you don't like any of the ones listed, don't worry! You have plenty more to choose from.

If you're building multiple cities and you want to connect them, you can use a bridge or a tunnel. Some players team up to build a city, and this strategy is almost always a great idea. Two heads are better than one, right? Together, you'll come up with even more ideas — and a better city.

Building something as large as a city takes time, but it's definitely worth it. Planning (in this case, making a blueprint) is the most important part of building a city, because it saves you time and effort later. If you don't plan, you may have to tear down and rebuild things, and your city won't look organized.

We like to use paper and pencil to make a blueprint before we start building. To get started, make a list of the buildings you need and sketch each one on paper to see which one should go where. If you plan to construct walls around your city, include them in your blueprint.

Don't reinvent the wheel — take a look at other players' cities to see which components they have and which ones you like and add those items to your own design.

You have a ton of choices when you build a city — so many different styles and layouts! You can have a modern city with roads and shops, or you can make a themed city (such as sports or medieval times).

If you want your city to be sports themed, add sports flags and colors to houses and buildings. Add basketball courts or baseball fields or even a soccer field.

Choosing whether you want city walls depends on the image you're aiming for. Walls excel as a defense against other players and mobs, but they make your city look closed off. On the other hand, without a wall, your city is open and defenseless. If you're in SinglePlayer mode, city walls keep out mobs that will likely spawn there.

While you're building the wall, finagle a way to get in and out! If you're making a decorative wall, arches make nice gateways; if the wall is mostly for defensive purposes, build a hidden doorway in the ground that drops you into a secret tunnel. (We show you how to do it later in this chapter.)

Whew! After all that planning, you can start building. We suggest building your city wall first because it's easy to make. A city wall is basically the same as a wall in a building — the main difference is height. The height depends on the wall's purpose. If you want to protect your city against other players or mobs, make the walls relatively high — at least five blocks high.

Next, start on your buildings. As you build, leave room for roads and paths — you need a way to get around town. You don't have to dig out the roads and paths yet; just use blocks as placeholders. We'll go over paths and roads in the next section. You can finish the roads and paths when the buildings are done.

Is it starting to look like a city? Fantastic! Now it's time to start decorating. Choose decorations that match your city's theme: If the city is modern, add roads, lampposts, and sidewalks. If the city is futuristic, add floating houses or lots of machines (see Chapter 6 for more on machines). You can also use water or lava to make the city truly exciting. Both can be nice to look at, and they provide a certain level of protection. If you end up adding water or lava, you need bridges (we talk about those in a minute) in order to get across them.

Ah, success! Your city is finished. Walk around and enjoy it!

Adding paths

Paths are truly handy because they're both decorative and useful. They can be small walkways or wide roads. Paths make cities and gardens look nice, but they also make it easy to find places or simply to move from Point A to Point B. Paths most commonly consist of dirt, paved road, or stone sidewalk.

If you're using paths as roads, figure out how long and how wide the road should be. Earlier, when we begin walking you through building a city, we encourage you to use blocks as placeholders for paths and roads. If you've already done that, you can easily see how wide and long they are.

If you didn't leave a space, don't worry; you can still make room for a path. Go ahead and look over your city. Is there enough space between houses and buildings for a path? If not, you may have to destroy a wall to make a building narrower. Even if there's enough room between buildings to make a road, take a minute to decide exactly where you want the road to go so that you don't end up tearing down too much of the city (or the wrong part of the city).

Follow the yellow brick road

To build a path, follow these instructions (the steps are the same whether you're building a road or a garden path):

1. **Dig out the rows of blocks where you want the road to be.**

   You can dig as deep as you want, but you only need to dig 1 block deep.

2. **Gather the materials you need for the path or road.**

   The type of material is up to you, but many people use cobblestone or stone brick. (The rest of this step list works with stone brick.)

3. **Place 4 stone blocks on the crafting table: 1 stone block in the left bottom box; 1 in the left middle box; 1 in the middle column bottom box; and 1 in the center box, as shown in Figure 4-6.**

   The crafting table changes those stones into brick.

Figure 4-6: Making stone bricks.

4. **Take the brick and place them into your inventory.**

5. **Repeat Steps 3 and 4 until you have all the bricks you need to build the path or road.**

6. **Take the bricks to the road, and place them in the holes you dug in Step 1.**

If you're not sure what to use for the paths and roads, think about what matches the theme of your town or city. If you have a village, keep it simple: Use sand or dirt. If you have a modern city, use black wool to resemble pavement, or obsidian. (The full-size book, *Minecraft For Dummies*, tells you how to dye wool.) If you're not sure how to get wool, don't worry! All you need is a sheep and a shear. To make a shear, you need 2 iron ingots. Place 1 iron ingot in the left row of the bottom box of the crafting table and the other in the center box. Take the shear that will appear in exchange for the iron ingots. After you have made a shear, find a sheep and use the shear to cut off the sheep's wool (right click on the sheep). This should give you 1 to 3 wools.

Though you can get real obsidian, it's difficult and dangerous when you're in Survival mode — that's why we suggest using wool to resemble the obsidian. Obsidian is usually only used for a path when you're in Creative Mode.

Real obsidian is gorgeous, though — it has a deep, rich color and texture. Many players think it's worth the trouble to get the real thing. You can get obsidian in two ways: Mine it or make it.

Mining obsidian is dangerous because, under the obsidian rock, you'll probably find lava. As you can imagine, falling into lava can be dangerous to your health. To avoid being killed by lava, mine a single obsidian block as a test to see whether lava is underneath it. If it is, you lose the block you just mined, because it falls into the lava and is destroyed — but that's better than dying.

The point here is that you're not interested in mining obsidian; what you're looking for is the lava. So, put to good use the lava you found, by carefully scooping up the lava with a bucket, carrying the bucket to the road, and then filling the hole with the lava. After you have the lava in place, fill the bucket with water and pour it on top of the lava — the mixture of lava and water makes obsidian.

If you think that the road is plain-looking, you can jazz it up with lampposts or glowstone. To make glowstone, you need 4 units of glowstone dust. You can get the dust in one of four ways:

- kill a witch — she can drop as many as 6 units of glowstone dust when she dies
- trade a villager for it
- break a glowstone — it will drop 4 units of glowstone dust
- harvest it from the Nether. (This is the easiest way to get glowstone dust.)

When you have 4 units of glowstone dust, you can easily make the glowstone. Place the 4 units of glowstone dust on the crafting table: one in the left bottom box; one in the left middle box; one in the middle lower box; and one in the center box. The craft table exchanges the glowstone dust for a lit glowstone. Repeat that process until you have as many glowstone as you need. You can then place the glowstones at strategic places along the road.

Make paths pretty

If you've made a garden path, you can embellish it with an entryway, such as an arch. To create an arch doorway, follow these steps:

1. **Make sure that you have 17 blocks of the same material that you used for your path.**

2. **Stack 5 blocks on top of each other.**

   If you want to build the arch higher than you can reach, jump (press the spacebar) and right-click to place a block underneath you. You can do this as many times as you need.

3. **Place 5 blocks side by side from the top of that stack, as shown in Figure 4-7.**

   Don't worry about blocks falling on your head — they hang suspended in the air while you build.

Figure 4-7: Building an arch.

4. **Starting at the other end of the horizontal row, build another vertical stack 5 blocks high, working from the top to the ground, as shown in Figure 4-8.**

5. **Place 1 block in the upper left corner of the arch's opening.**

Figure 4-8: A basic archway.

> **6. Place 1 block in the upper right corner of the arch's opening.**

Figure 4-9 shows a finished archway.

Figure 4-9: A finished archway for your garden. Nice sunset!

Congratulations! You've successfully made an archway.

Building bridges

Bridges are fun. You can use them for their normal functions, such as moving across bodies of water or lava or making it easy for others to enter your city. Or you can think of new ways to use bridges, such as making a sky bridge between buildings.

As with most components of Minecraft, you have many options for creating bridges. Some bridges have a purpose (such as getting you from Point A to Point B), others are built purely for decoration, and still others do both — get you where you need to go while looking good doing it.

Bridges that are purely functional (such as getting you or another player from Point A to Point B) are called *simple bridges*, and, you guessed it, they're easy to make. But that doesn't mean they have to be boring! You can add decorations such as waterfalls or glowstone lighting for some extra flair. (More on that later.)

As when you build a building, a city, or a path, be sure to do some planning before you start. Figure out where you want the bridge to take people, how wide and long the bridge needs to be, and whether you want to build a regular bridge somewhere in the city or a sky bridge. When you know this information, you can tell how many blocks you need to get the job done — the number of blocks you need depends on how long and wide you want the bridge. If you want to be exact, make a wire frame of the bridge. (For more on wireframes, see Chapter 5.)

Next, choose and gather your materials based on what you like. (Make sure to gather as much as you need to build the whole bridge!)

If you want the bridge to be a little flashier, you can choose golden blocks, such as glowstone. If you're shooting for a more traditional bridge, choose gray blocks, such as cobblestone or brick stone.

To get started with your first simple bridge, lay down as many blocks as you need to make the width of the bridge. For example, if you want the bridge to be 4 blocks wide, place 4 blocks at the base of Point A and continue putting bricks down until you reach Point B.

If you're building a sky bridge, you might be worried about falling off the bridge as you build it. You can avoid that concern by moving slower (press and hold Shift) as you build. Walk to the edge of the block you're standing on, and place another block in front of it. Keep going until you've made the sky bridge long enough.

Make sidewalls on any bridge so that you and others don't fall off while crossing it. To make sidewalls on both regular and sky bridges, stack blocks along the outer rows of the bridge, as shown in Figure 4-10. The height of the walls is up to you, but keep them low if you want to be able to see over the sides — 1 block high should be fine.

Figure 4-10: The sidewalls of a bridge

Sometimes, you might like to put a roof over your bridge. A roof helps protect you from the weather, and it's a nice decorative touch. Making a roof for a bridge is similar to making a ceiling for a house or building.

To build a roof, stand on a sidewall and make a vertical stack of blocks. (You decide how high). From the top of this stack, build a straight line of blocks away from the stack until you get to the other side of the bridge. For an example of a roof, look to Figure 4-11.

Figure 4-11: A roof for your bridge

To add a waterfall to the bridge, get a bucket and fill it with water. Right-click to place the water on a block that is part of, or near, the bridge. Figure 4-12 shows an example of a bridge with a waterfall.

Figure 4-12: A bridge with a waterfall

To make a bucket, you need 3 iron ingots. Place 1 ingot in the middle box in the left column, another ingot in the bottom box of the middle column, and the third ingot in the middle box of the right column. Then take the bucket in exchange for the 3 ingots.

Using Passageways

"Passageways" is just a fancy way of saying hallways and tunnels. In the next few sections you'll find out how to build both.

Hallways

You have hallways in your house, right? You have them in Minecraft, too. You can build a hallway with any type of block, but for this example we are going to use wooden planks. The number of blocks you need depends on how long you want your hallway to be.

After you have your materials, it's time to start building! First, build the walls of your hallway — it's just like building a wall of a house. Stack blocks until you have a wall that is the appropriate height. Simple, right?

Here's the main thing to remember when you're building a hallway: Make it big enough for you to fit through! The smallest hallway you can have is 2 blocks tall and 1 block wide. If you want to make your hallway larger, knock yourself out. You may want a larger hallway if you want to feel like you have more room and aren't in a confined space.

Now, you just have to build the ceiling, then you're done! For more information on how to build a ceilings, check out the "Starting the Build" section, earlier in the chapter.

Tunnels

Tunnels are an easy way to connect two areas of your city. They're also used for underground mining. Tunnels don't have to be on land — you can make underwater tunnels, too. (Awesome, right?)

You don't need specific tools to dig a tunnel, but depending on how deep you plan to dig, a pickaxe and shovel might be helpful. (See the "Tunnel mining" section, later in this chapter for more info.) To dig, just left click. Depending on what you're using your tunnel for, you can dig straight down or change directions. For example, if you want to make a tunnel that goes from your house to another building, you can dig down, then change direction and keep digging your tunnel toward the other building.

Before you start digging, however, you need to make some ladders so you can return to the surface. To make a ladder, you need 7 sticks. To make sticks, place 1 wooden plank in the center box and another in the box below it. Doing so gets you 4 sticks, so you'll need to do this twice. After you have 7 sticks, place all of them on the crafting table, filling the left and right columns. Place the last stick in the center box. Take the 3 ladders you get for the sticks. The ladders will help you get into and out of your tunnel.

You can dig down as far as you want, but the farther you dig, the more ladders or stairs you'll need to make to come back up.

Trapdoors

When you dig a tunnel, you need to install a trapdoor so no one accidentally falls into it. To build a trapdoor, follow these simple steps:

1. **Gather 2 regular wood and place them in the crafting table (any box will do).**

   The crafting table exchanges the 2 regular wood for 8 wooden planks. (They look like a block.)

2. **Place the wooden planks on the crafting table, filling the bottom two rows.**

   The crafting table exchanges the planks for 2 trapdoors.

3. **Take the 2 trapdoors and place them into your inventory.**

4. **Place one trapdoor over the hole leading to the tunnel.**

   Right click to open your trapdoor.

Tunnel mining

Tunnel mining (also known as *branch mining*) is an easy way to find and obtain valuable ore. It works like this: You dig a main tunnel then dig smaller tunnels off to the sides. This arrangement kind of looks like a tree, with the main tunnel as the trunk and the smaller tunnels as the branches. The main tunnel is like your home base — all your smaller tunnels lead back to it, which means you're less likely to get lost!

When you dig your main tunnel, make sure it's tall and wide. After that you can start digging your branches. Dig one branch at a time and mine for ore as you go. If you don't find the resources you want, go back to the main tunnel and start another branch.

Make sure not to mine straight down — you don't want to fall into the opening of a lava pool and die.

When deciding where to mine, pick a low-lying place — nothing too high. To make sure mobs can't enter your mine, build dirt walls around it — don't forget to add a door! (See Figure 4-13.) Another option is to enclose your area with a wooden fence (see Chapter 6).

Figure 4-13: Securing a mine using only some dirt and a door.

To create a mining tunnel, you need a pickaxe, a shovel, ladders, and lots of torches. This section gives you the instructions for each of these tasks. (Okay, we lied — the ladder instructions are in the earlier section, "Tunnels.")

To make a pickaxe, you need 2 sticks and 3 wooden planks. (If you have no sticks on hand, you can make them by using another set of 2 wooden planks. Just place the wooden planks in the center and lower middle boxes of the crafting table. The crafting table does the rest.)

Place the planks in the top three boxes of the crafting table. Then place one stick in the middle box of the bottom row and 1 stick in the center box. Take the pickaxe in exchange for the sticks and wooden planks.

To make a shovel, you need 1 wooden plank and 2 sticks. Place the 1 stick in the middle box of the bottom row and 1 stick in the center box. Then place the plank in the middle box of the top row.

Instead of using wooden planks when making a pickaxe or shovel, you can use cobblestone, iron ingots, gold ingots, or diamond — all of them are stronger than planks.

When mining, bring wood to make torches. As you mine, you'll find more than enough coal to make torches.

To make a torch, you need 2 wooden planks and 1 coal. Turn the 2 planks into sticks by placing them on your inventory crafting table, filling the top and bottom boxes. Exchange the planks for the sticks. Place 1 stick in the bottom box of your inventory crafting table, then place the coal in the box above it. Take the lit torch in exchange for the stick and coal. Make as many torches as you can before you begin mining.

Secret Rooms

Have you ever wished for a secret room? Well, now you can make one! Minecraft has two types of secret rooms: below ground and above ground. To see an example of the two types, look at Figure 4-14.

A below ground secret room is at the end of a tunnel. An above ground secret room is at the end of a hallway. And since you've already learned how to make both a tunnel and a hallway, you're halfway there!

Figure 4-14: The two types of secret rooms: below ground (left), and above ground (right).

Making a secret room is easy; you just need to know how big you want it to be. If you plan to use the room to store items such as chests, food items, weapons, and tools, the room can probably be relatively small. But if the room will be a retreat or resemble a library, it needs to be larger.

It doesn't really matter whether your secret room is above or below ground; you make them the same way. The only difference is that below ground you break blocks (left click) and above ground you place blocks (right click).

The instructions below work for both (just break or place blocks as needed). Here's how to make a square room:

1. **At the end of your tunnel or hallway break/place blocks straight ahead to make one side of the room.**

   Break or place blocks until the room is as long as you want it to be. If the length is 15 blocks, for example, break or place 15 blocks straight in front of you.

2. **Make the next side of the room.**

   Turn to one side or the other and make another wall for the width of your room. But this time you're going to stop one block short of the number of blocks you want for your width. For example, if you want your width to be 15 blocks, only break or place 14 blocks.

3. **Turn again to make the third side of the room.**

   Break or place one less block than the intended length. So if you the first wall you made was 15 blocks, break or place 14 blocks for this wall.

4. **Turn one last time to make the final side of the room.**

   Again, break or place one less block (as noted in steps 2 and 3). Figure 4-15 shows what the outline of your secret room looks like.

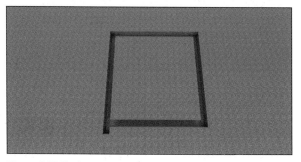

Figure 4-15: You're on your way to having your own secret room!

5. If your room is underground: Dig out the middle part of the room.

If you build your secret room above ground, you will be able to see the addition from the outside of your building. For example, if you have a square building, your new room will probably stick out from the rest of the building (like the one in Figure 4-16).

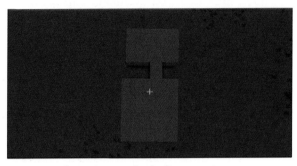

Figure 4-16: A secret room that isn't so secret.

You can camouflage the new room by placing blocks in the telltale spots around it until the building looks normal again. (See Figure 4-17 to see what we mean.)

Figure 4-17: There! You can't even tell there's a secret room.

Now, your secret room is ready for you to decorate any way you please. Chapters 5 and 6 can give you ideas about decorating.

If you made your secret room underground, are you wondering how to get back up? You can get in and out of the tunnel by using either the same ladders you used to build the tunnel or a staircase.

Stairs can be a hassle — not because they're hard to make (they're not), but because you have to jump to use them. And jumping requires a high ceiling so that you don't keep banging your head. It's a lot easier to just use a ladder.

If you'd really rather use a staircase, you can make one from wooden planks, cobblestone, brick, Nether brick, stone brick, sandstone, or quartz block. You can find out how to build a staircase in Chapter 6; here, we want to show you how to make a block staircase:

1. **Dig 1 block in the wall in front of you and 1 block above it.**

   Now you have a vertical hole that's 2 blocks high.

2. **Walk into the hole.**

3. **Break the block directly above you.**

4. **Break the block that is at your eye level.**

5. **Break the block above the one that you just broke. This creates a hole that is two blocks high.**

6. **Jump into the hole that you just created.**

7. **Repeat Steps 4-6 until you have reached the surface.**

There you go! You have finished your secret room and tunnel.

5

The Art of Minecraft Design

*Y*our Minecraft space is a reflection of you — your personality, your likes and dislikes, your creativity, and so on. Everything you design shows a different part of your imagination. To put your best foot forward, try to master a few basic design principles — such as symmetry (balancing the design) and the correct color choice — to make a big difference in your buildings, both inside and outside.

If you choose to read this entire chapter, you'll know how to make a plan for your new building, use symmetry to make everything interesting, make all kinds of colors, and create cool-looking floors, walls, and roofs.

Balancing the Design

People like to look at objects that are orderly and balanced. One way to achieve a sense of order and balance is to rely on *symmetry,* where elements on one side of a real (or imaginary) line are paired with elements on the other side of that line. Check out Figure 5-1, where we've added a real line down the center of the image. Note that each element on one side of the line has an exact match on the other side of the line — that's symmetry.

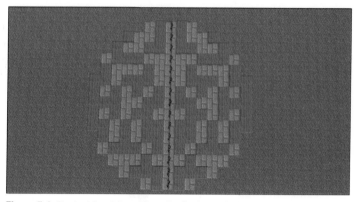

Figure 5-1: Each side of the object that's shown is the same.

There are two types of symmetry: even and odd. *Even* symmetry is based around even numbers — 2, 4, 6, 8, and so on. An even symmetrical structure can be divided into two equal groups of blocks. For example, if you make a wall 4 blocks or 8 blocks wide, the wall has even symmetry. Figure 5-2 shows how even symmetry looks inside a room.

Figure 5-2: A room with even symmetry.

Though even symmetry looks nice and orderly, it makes decorating a bit of a challenge. Even symmetry makes centering decorations in a room (lights and paintings, for example) somewhat difficult. If a decoration is placed on the line of symmetry (in Figure 5-2, this line is along the length of the table), it must be an even number of blocks wide. Suppose that you want to place a chandelier on the ceiling of the room shown in Figure 5-2. To place the chandelier in the exact center of the room, you need to make the chain at least 2 blocks thick, which can look quite strange for decorations of this sort. If you don't want the decoration to mess up the symmetry, you have to make two decorations and place one on either side of the room, or make two of the decorations and hang them together.

Odd symmetry occurs when you use an odd number of blocks to build an object (such as making a wall 3 blocks or 7 blocks wide). Some of the blocks are then along the line of symmetry rather than on one side or another. We've found that odd symmetry works well for most design choices — centering decorations, making shapes, or making objects look more realistic, for example.

If you want to make a fountain look smooth and realistic, for example, you should use one bucket of water (producing odd symmetry) instead of two. When you use 2 squares of water (even symmetry), the fountain starts to look bulky and weird. Figure 5-3 shows two fountains: one with odd symmetry (on the right) and one with even symmetry (on the left).

Figure 5-3: The same decoration, with two different types of symmetry.

If you want to use shapes in your designs, you should know that most of them require odd symmetry. For example, if you want to make a hexagon (you can find out how in Chapter 9), you need an odd number of blocks for the straight sides so that the angles line up the right way.

Adding Color to Your Builds

Can you imagine how boring a game would be if it didn't have color? Yuck. Color makes everything much more interesting — especially when you're building and decorating. You can use color to express your personality; make your house look artistic and edgy or more traditional; or even subtly define its purpose, as in these examples:

- **Dark colors** create gloomy or ominous environments, like mysterious underground rooms or sinister castles.

- **Pale colors** look light, sterile, or ethereal — you can use them to build objects such as palaces, factories, or temples.

- **Bright colors** are powerful and cheerful, but sometimes look unrealistic. You can use them to construct objects such as tapestries and amusement parks.

- **Red colors** can create hot environments or cheerful settings, from volcanoes to amusement parks.

- **Blue colors** bring to mind sky and water — you might use them to build floating castles or underwater hideouts.

- **Green colors** look natural and work well with gardens or greeneries.

However, note that these are just suggestions and if you have a good idea for colors you want to incorporate into your build, then just pick those colors.

Understanding how colors work together

In Minecraft, as in the real world, you basically have three main color groups, as in these examples:

- **Cold hues:** Blue, green, and purple

- **Warm hues:** Red, orange, and yellow

- **Neutral hues:** Black, white, gray, and brown

You can use any color any way you want, wherever you want, but (for most eyes) certain combinations look better than others. Putting too many contrasting colors together can be distracting. For example, putting cold and warm colors next to each other can look odd — and even ugly (depending on how bright the colors are). If you want to place cold and warm colors together, use a neutral color, too, to break up the contrast a bit to make it feel a bit more natural.

For example, using blue and red stained clay together looks strange unless they're balanced by a neutral color. For another example, check out Figure 5-4. You can see two (very different) buildings. The brick building pairs the red brick with brown corner columns (the colors complement each other). The other building uses lots of colors that don't quite work well together.

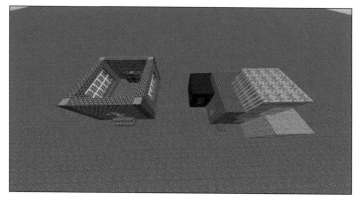

Figure 5-4: Use colors that complement each other, as in the building on the left.

If you want to use color in your buildings, you have to either gather blocks of the colors you want or craft them yourself. (Some of these blocks spawn naturally, and others have to be crafted or smelted.) The next few sections tell you how to create some of these blocks and how to craft and mix dyes to produce any color you want.

Crafting and mixing dyes

One of the easiest ways to craft blocks of certain colors is with *dyes*. Though these items cannot be placed like blocks, they can be used to craft colored wool, stained glass, and stained clay.

You can choose from 16 different dyes, each of which produces a different color. Table 5-1 describes how to craft each dye.

Table 5-1		Dyes
Dye	*Color*	*How to Obtain It*
Bone meal	White	Craft it from bones.
Cactus green	Green	Cook a cactus block in a furnace.
Cocoa beans	Brown	Destroy cocoa bean pods in the jungle.
Cyan dye	Cyan	Craft green and blue dyes together.
Dandelion yellow	Yellow	Craft it from dandelions or sunflowers.
Gray dye	Gray	Craft black and white dyes together.
Ink sac	Black	Obtain it from squids.
Lapis lazuli	Blue	Mine lapis lazuli ore.
Light blue dye	Light blue	Craft it from blue orchids or by crafting blue and white dyes together.
Light gray dye	Light gray	Craft it from azure bluets, oxeye daisies, or white tulips or by combining 2 white dyes and 1 black dye. You can also simply craft a gray dye and a white dye together.
Lime dye	Lime	Craft green and white dyes together.
Magenta dye	Magenta	Craft it from lilacs or alliums or by combining 2 reds, 1 blue, and 1 white. You can also craft a purple dye and a pink dye together.
Orange dye	Orange	Craft it from orange tulips or by crafting red dyes and yellow dyes together.
Pink dye	Pink	Craft it from peonies or pink tulips or by crafting red dyes and white dyes together.
Purple dye	Purple	Craft red dyes and blue dyes together.
Rose red	Red	Crafted from poppies, roses, or red tulips.

Many colorful blocks are not obtained by dyeing wool, clay, or glass, however. We cover them in the following sections.

Making cold-color materials

Blue, green, and purple are *cold* colors. Table 5-2 lists all the blocks you can make that have cold colors, as well as the ingredients and special cultivating tactics needed to make them.

Table 5-2	Cold-Colored Materials	
Material	*Ingredients*	*Special Cultivating Tactics*
Lapis lazuli ore	Grey and blue	Spawns in caves and can be gathered only in its pure form with the Silk Touch enchantment
Lapis lazuli block	Blue	None
Diamond ore	Grey and light blue	Spawns in caves and can be gathered only in its pure form with the Silk Touch enchantment
Diamond block	Light blue	None
Emerald ore	Grey and green	Spawns in caves and can be gathered only in its pure form with the Silk Touch enchantment
Emerald block	Green	None
Light blue wool	Light blue	None
Cyan wool	Cyan	None
Blue wool	Blue	None
Lime wool	Lime	None
Green wool	Green	None
Magenta wool	Magenta	None
Grass block	Green and brown	Spawns naturally on top of the land and spreads to nearby dirt blocks

(continued)

Table 5-2 *(continued)*

Material	Ingredients	Special Cultivating Tactics
Spruce leaves	Green	Spawns in spruce trees and has to be gathered with shears
Jungle leaves	Green	Spawns in jungle trees and has to be gathered with shears
Birch leaves	Olive-green	Spawns in birch trees and has to be gathered with shears
Melon	Green	Grown from melon seeds
Cactus	Green with block dots	Found in deserts
Blue stained glass	Blue	None
Light blue stained Glass	Light blue	None
Lime stained glass	Lime	None
Green stained glass	Green	None
Purple stained glass	Purple	None
Magenta stained glass	Magenta	None
Blue stained glass pane	Blue	None
Light blue stained glass pane	Light blue	None
Lime stained glass pane	Lime	None
Green stained glass pane	Green	None
Purple stained glass pane	Purple	None
Magenta stained glass pane	Magenta	None

Material	Ingredients	Special Cultivating Tactics
End stone	Very light green	Must be found in the End (though, fortunately, almost the entire End is made of end stone)
Beacon	Light blue	None
Ender chest	Dark blue	None
Packed ice	Light blue	Can be found only in the rare Ice Spikes biome.
Ice	Light blue	Can be found in cold biomes in place of water
Blue stained clay	Blue	None
Light blue stained clay	Light blue	None
Lime stained clay	Lime	None
Green stained clay	Green	None
Purple stained clay	Purple	None
Mossy cobblestone	Green and grey	Spawns in jungle temples and spawned rooms
Mossy stone brick	Green and grey	Can also be found in strongholds
Mossy cobblestone wall	Green and grey	None
Slime block	Green	None
Primaries	Turquoise	Can be found in underwater temples
Primaries bricks	Turquoise	Can be found in underwater temples
Dark prismarine	Dark turquoise	Can also be found in underwater temples
Sea lamps	Very light blue	Can be found in underwater temples

Making warm-color materials

If you want to use warm colors instead, red, yellow, and orange are good ways to go. Table 5-3 lists the warm-color materials you can make as well as the ingredients and special cultivating tactics needed to make them.

Table 5-3	Warm-Colored Blocks	
Material	*Ingredients*	*Special Cultivating Tactics*
Granite	None	Spawns randomly underground
Polished granite	Four granite	None
Acacia wood planks	One acacia wood	None
Red sand	None	Spawns in the Mesa biome
Gold ore	None	Can be found underground at levels 32 and below
Iron ore	None	Can be found anywhere underground
Sponge	Wet sponge	Cooked in a furnace
Wet sponge	None	Can be found in sea temples or dropped by elder guardians
Sandstone	Four sand	Can be found in layers underneath sand in the deserts as well as in desert temples
Chiseled sandstone	Two sandstone slabs	Can be found in desert temples
Smooth sandstone	Four sandstone or chiseled sandstone	Can be found in desert temples
Sandstone slab	Three sandstone	
Red wool	One wool and 1 red dye	None

Material	Ingredients	Special Cultivating Tactics
Orange wool	One wool and 1 orange dye	None
Yellow wool	One wool and 1 yellow dye	None
Pink wool	One wool and 1 pink dye	None
Gold block	Nine gold ingots	None
Brick slab	Three brick blocks	None
Nether brick slab	Three nether bricks	None
Brick block	Four bricks	None
Bookshelf	Six wood and 3 books	None
Redstone ore	None	Found underground at Levels 16 and below
Redstone block	Nine redstone	None
Netherrack	None	Can be found everywhere in the Nether
Pumpkin	None	Can be found anywhere aboveground except in Desert and Mesa biomes
Jack-o'-lantern	One torch and 1 pumpkin	None
Glowstone	Four glowstone dust	Can be found in the Nether
Red stained glass	Eight glass and 1 red dye	None
Orange stained glass	Eight glass and 1 orange dye	None
Yellow stained glass	Eight glass and 1 yellow dye	None
Pink stained glass	Eight glass and 1 pink dye	None
Red stained glass pane	Six red stained glass	None

(continued)

Table 5-3 *(continued)*

Material	Ingredients	Special Cultivating Tactics
Orange stained glass pane	Six orange stained glass	None
Yellow stained glass pane	Six yellow stained glass	None
Pink stained glass pane	Six pink stained glass	None
Brick stairs	Six bricks	None
Redstone lamp	Four redstone and 1 glowstone	None
Acacia wood slab	Three acacia wood planks	None
Jungle wood slab	Three jungle wood planks	None
Nether quartz	None	Can be found in patches in the Nether and must be mined with Silk Touch enchantment
Red stained clay	Eight hardened clay and 1 red dye	Can be found in Mesa biomes
Orange stained clay	Eight hardened clay and 1 orange dye	Can be found in Mesa biomes
Yellow stained clay	Eight hardened clay and 1 yellow dye	Can be found in Mesa biomes
Pink stained clay	Eight hardened clay and 1 pink dye	Can be found in Mesa biomes
Acacia wood stairs	Six acacia wood planks	None
Jungle wood stairs	Six jungle wood planks	None
Hay block	Nine wheat	None

Making neutral-color materials

Whether you simply like neutral colors or you want to use them to break up the contrast of other colors, gray, black, white, and brown are good colors to have around. Table 5-4 lists the neutral-color materials you can make, as well as the ingredients and special cultivating tactics needed to make them.

Table 5-4	Neutral-Colored Blocks	
Material	**Ingredients**	**Special Cultivating Tactic**
Stone	Cobblestone	Heat in a furnace; can be found everywhere underground but must be mined using the Silk Touch enchantment
Cobblestone	None	Dropped when stone is broken
Diorite	None	Can be found in patches underground
Polished diorite	Four diorite	None
Andesite	None	Can be found in patches underground
Polished andesite	Four andesite	None
Stone brick	Four stone	Can be found throughout strongholds
Cracked stone brick	Stone bricks	Heat in a furnace; can be found in strongholds
Chiseled stone brick	Two stone brick slabs	Can be found in strongholds
Stone slab	Three stone	None

(continued)

Table 5-4 *(continued)*

Material	Ingredients	Special Cultivating Tactic
Cobblestone slab	Three cobblestone	None
Stone brick slab	Three bricks	None
Oak wood planks	One oak wood	Can sometimes be found in witch huts
Oak wood	None	Can be found in oak trees
Spruce wood planks	One spruce wood	None
Spruce wood	None	Can be found in spruce trees
Birch wood plank	One birch wood	None
Birch wood	None	Can be found in birch trees
Dark oak wood planks	One dark oak wood	None
Dark oak wood	None	Can be found in dark oak trees
Jungle wood planks	One jungle wood	None
Jungle wood	None	Can be found in jungle trees
Acacia wood	None	Can be found in acacia trees
Oak wood slabs	Three oak wood planks	None
Spruce wood slabs	Three spruce wood planks	None
Birch wood slabs	Three birch wood planks	None
Dark oak wood slabs	Three dark oak wood planks	None
Jungle wood slabs	Three jungle wood planks	None
Fence	Six sticks	None

Material	Ingredients	Special Cultivating Tactic
Fence gate	Four sticks and 2 of any type of wood	None
Cobblestone wall	Six cobblestone	None
Iron bars	Six iron ingots	None
Coal block	Nine coal	None
Iron block	Nine iron ingots	None
Glass	Sand	Melt sand in a furnace
Stained glass	Eight glass and 1 neutral-colored dye	None
Glass pane	Six glass	None
End stone	None	Can be found everywhere in the End
End portal	None	Blocks are located in the End portal frame located in the Stronghold
Clay	None	Found underwater near beaches
Hardened clay	Clay	Bake in a furnace; also located in a layer of the Mesa biome
Stained clay	Eight hardened clay and 1 neutral color	None
White wool	Four string	Sheer or kill white sheep
Colored wool	One wool and 1 dye	None
Block of quartz	Four quartz	None
Chiseled quartz block	Two quartz slabs	None
Pillar quartz block	Two blocks of quartz	None
Quartz slab	Three blocks of quartz	None

(continued)

Table 5-4 *(continued)*

Material	Ingredients	Special Cultivating Tactic
Obsidian	None	Forms naturally whenever water meets lava source blocks; solid obsidian pillars can also be found in the End
Note block	Eight wood and 1 redstone	None
Juke box	One diamond and 8 wood	None
Chest	Eight wood	Can be found in dungeons, desert temples, and jungle temples

Wireframing the Build

A *wireframe* is a temporary outline of a building — kind of a sample building — made of easy-to-break blocks, like dirt. Wireframes are handy because they help you see whether your original plan needs a tweak or two and let you estimate how many blocks you need for the final build.

A wireframe helps you see how your building will look with different floor plans and features. If you decide that you don't like a particular look, you can easily change it by breaking down a section and moving blocks around until you come up with a design you like.

The layout of your building is important. If you don't like it now and you decide to change it later, you may run into problems. Now is a good time to experiment with curves, varying floor and wall heights, ceilings, and roofs.

1. **Using dirt blocks, outline the base of the structure.**

   Figure 5-5 shows an example of a wireframe we made and then decided to change.

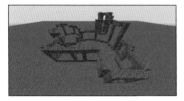

Figure 5-5: Outlining the structure.

2. Using more dirt blocks, outline the structure's walls.

This step helps you estimate how high the walls should be. If you thought you wanted the walls to be 5 blocks high but the wireframe shows that it looks better with 7 blocks, you can make a note of it when you're building the structure. Figure 5-6 shows an example of wire-framed walls.

Figure 5-6: Provisionally adding walls.

3. Revise, if needed.

After the floor and walls are outlined, you should have a good idea of what the structure will look like. While the structure is still easy to edit, go back and change anything that doesn't look right.

Don't forget the extras. Go ahead and wireframe anything you want to include in and around the building, such as bridges and paths. Be sure to make good use of your wireframe when referencing your project when you actually start building your structure.

Customizing Floors, Roofs, and Walls

You can't really have a building without some basics — floors, roofs, and walls are what make a building a building, right? You can build some basic objects, but why not make them truly interesting and cool?

Adding pizazz to floors

Plain floors made from a single kind of block are dull. To add a little "oomph" to your rooms, use a variety of stones to make a path, pattern, or symbol. A floor with a checkerboard pattern or a zombie face on it would really grab a visitor's attention!

If you want to cover a floor with a tiled pattern, in other words a pattern that iterates itself across the floor, follow these steps:

1. **Create an interesting tile that's a bit on the smaller side.**

   Arrange some blocks that work well together, but make the tile small enough that 9 or more of them can fit in the room. You can make carpets, wood, quartz, or anything else. (Figure 5-7 gives a few examples.)

Figure 5-7: Floor tiling examples.

2. **Outline a room large enough to fit the tiles comfortably inside.**

   The room should be just large enough that the tiles can neatly fit inside. For example, if you're using 5x5 tiles, you can fit them in a 20x25 room.

3. **Put the tiles together.**

   Starting from one corner, build the tile repeatedly inside the room until the entire floor is covered.

Making walls stand out

The fun stuff isn't limited to floor designs. Using blocks to make patterns in the wall (see the wall on the left in Figure 5-8) or adding slabs to make a 3D design (see the wall on the right in Figure 5-8) can add to the wow factor.

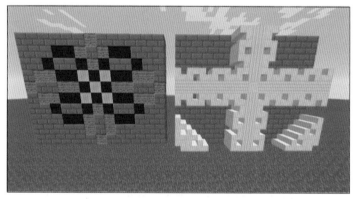

Figure 5-8: A couple of interesting walls.

To make a nice pattern in the wall, add in different kinds of blocks as you build, as spelled out in this step list:

1. **Choose a set of similar blocks.**

   Select blocks that look similar and have similar textures. Avoid objects such as slabs and stairs when the wall is 1 block thick.

2. **Create an interesting shape or pattern.**

   Use one of the blocks to create the centerpiece of the pattern, and fill the rest of the wall with your other blocks.

3. **Make corrections until you create the pattern you want.**

   Don't worry if you don't get it right the first time. After you finish the wall, you can easily spot any areas that look out of place — and then fix them.

If you want to go for it, you can make a 3D wall (refer to the wall on the right in Figure 5-8). Generally speaking, a 3D wall starts with a regular run-of-the-mill wall, but then you add slabs and stairs. These blocks can be crafted with wood, cobblestone, stone bricks, and the slabs can be crafted with smoothstone. These can make your design stick out a little from the original wall.

For specific instructions on creating a 3D wall, check out these steps:

1. **Build the backboard for the wall.**

   A 3D wall has a front and a back — so what do you want to appear in the back? You don't need to put lots of effort into this step, because a tiny portion of this backboard is visible. However, think about what sort of block you want to see through the foreground.

2. **Create a pattern primarily from slabs, stairs, and other blocks containing cutouts.**

   The idea here is to place blocks close enough together to act as a wall but that "wall" needs to contain a number of holes through which you can see the backboard.

3. **Make corrections until you create the pattern you want.**

   The backboard should be moderately visible throughout the wall. If a part of the wall looks weird or wrong, revise some of the blocks in the foreground.

A 3D wall takes up more space, so use them outside or in a large room.

Putting a lid on it

You don't have quite as many options for making a roof stand out. You're basically limited to manipulating its shape. You can make three kinds of roofs:

- **Short:** Made from half-slabs, short roofs are the easiest to customize — you can vary the shape and even make awesome roof shapes such as domes or waves. How cool would it be to have a beach house with a wave roof?

- **Flat:** Flat roofs are about as simple as it gets. The good news is that they work well for cabins and the like. The bad news is that they're so simple to make that just about the only way to spice one up is to add support beams or a pattern. You build flat roofs using slabs (or similar items).

- **Slanted:** Slanted roofs are okay by themselves, but they're most interesting when you use them with other types of roofs. Slanted roofs are made with stairs.

To build a roof that converges at the top, as just described, follow these steps:

1. **Build the base of the roof.**

    It's normally just a rectangular or rounded outline — a house without a ceiling.

2. **Create another group of blocks, but make sure that the blocks are slightly smaller in width than the blocks used to create the base walls. In other words, try to make it so that the next layer on the roof gets slowly smaller.**

3. **Starting on the topmost row of the base walls, place a row of l blocks flush against the row's inner edge.**

    This group is just large enough to fit neatly inside the base, but it is also higher up. It creates a staggered look, like a series of small steps meant to lead up to the peak of the roof.

4. **Repeat Steps 2 and 3 as needed.**

    The roofs shown in Figure 5-9 are made of many layers stacked on top of each other, each slightly smaller than the one below. No matter what the shape of the roof is, you can use this technique to build it easily.

Figure 5-9: Roofing examples.

6
Managing Your Space

In This Chapter
- Creating a floor plan and building the structure
- Decorating the inside and outside of your building
- Incorporating useful items into the architecture

*C*reating a building can be difficult if you're not sure what you want. This chapter not only helps you decide *what* you want to build but also shows you (step by step) *how* to create it. That means you can soon create your own floor plan and come up with ways to fill up the room exactly how you want. You can also build fully functional machines and farms while making the structure look good.

Getting In on the Ground Floor

Creating a building gives you the opportunity to let your creative imagination run wild, because you can create virtually anything — a house, a shop, or even an entire city.

Getting ready to build

We say, "Let your creative imagination run wild," but it's still important to think about what you want to build. Ask yourself what you want to accomplish with your building. Do you need shelter for yourself? Or do you want to create an interesting structure? You can add levels, new rooms, or almost anything else you can think of! Look at your surroundings and the amount of space you have. Will everything fit?

Now think about what you want your building to have. Do you want multiple rooms inside your structure? How about a balcony on the roof? Do you know what kinds of blocks you need to build everything? Make sure that you have an idea of what furniture you want inside your building, too. You don't want to finish your building, then realize that your room is too small for the furniture.

When you have a clear idea of what you're going for, you can start creating the floor plan. One way to do that is to draw the plan on paper — just like the blueprints real architects use — to get an idea of how the structure will look. This way, you can tweak your building before you make it, so you won't have to tweak it afterwards.

Basic building

Now, it's time to start building! First, gather the materials that you need. At this point, the only materials you'll need are the blocks that you want your building to be made of. Then, start building a wireframe of your building. For more information on wireframes, check out Chapter 5.

After you've finished your wireframe, start on the walls of your building. To build a wall, just stack blocks on top of each other and next to each other until you have a wall. After the walls are completed, build the ceiling, and you're done!

If you're having trouble building a ceiling because it's too high to work on, build yourself stairs so that you can climb up; you can always break (left click) stairs when you're done with the ceiling, if you want.

Building stairs is easy. All you have to do is place one block in front of you. Jump (spacebar) on that block, and then place two blocks in front of you. Continue doing this, adding one more block in front of you each time until you reach the top of your wall.

Make the ceiling a comfortable height. Two blocks high is a shallow ceiling, and 3 blocks gives you plenty of room to move around and jump.

Be sure to keep some open space inside the building. You don't want to make the rooms too cramped, because then it would be difficult to move around and place other objects inside the room.

For more information on building a building, look back to Chapter 4.

When you're done building, step back and inspect your work. Is this what you want? Did it turn out the way you thought it would? If not, see whether you can find the difference between the building on paper and the building you built.

Unleashing Your Interior Decorator

After you complete the outside of the building, it's time to turn your attention to the inside. You have just as much creative freedom inside as you do outside. It's completely up to you.

If you're not sure about what to put inside the building, ask yourself these questions:

- **Does the building have a specific theme?** If so, try to pick objects and decorations that apply to that theme. For example, if you wanted your building to look futuristic, try adding some glowstone your design.

- **Do you need any necessities?** For example, if you're in Survival mode, creating a workbench or a stove is helpful.

- **Why did you create the building?** If you originally wanted the building to be a library, for example, it makes sense to put bookshelves on the walls.

If you still have no idea what you should do about decorating your room, don't worry! We'll be talking more about decorations later in the chapter.

Keeping interiors light and airy

Sure, you want your room to be nicely decorated, but you don't want it to be cramped. To avoid this problem, place items in a room only if they truly belong there. For example, an oven belongs in a kitchen, and a bookcase belongs in a library. Keeping items in their (proper) places makes the room look like it belongs and serves a purpose while staying open and comfortable.

In Minecraft, nothing is set in stone. If you feel that the structure is starting to look dark and cramped rather than light and airy, you're not stuck with the original design: Just make the rooms larger! That happens all the time — your original plan may have called for a small room, but now that it's built, you're not so sure it was the best idea. That's okay! A lot of things change between the original idea and the actual building. If you have this problem, try breaking (left click) the original walls and rebuild them a little farther away, making the room larger. This way, you have more room to place decorations and objects without the room being too cramped.

Using empty space effectively

After putting the finishing touches on a building, you'll likely discover that it still has a lot of empty space left inside. That's okay, because you wouldn't want the building to be too cramped.

However, if the building has *too* much empty space, it looks unfinished. It's good to have room to move around, but if you have too much, the room starts looking like a cheap motel room — and you don't want that!

Consider again why you set out to build this room. Does it have a specific purpose? If so, try to choose an appropriate piece of furniture or decoration for that purpose. If the room is a kitchen, for example, its "purpose" is tied up with preparing and serving food. To better carry out that purpose, you need an oven (or two) as well as countertops (easily made using blocks and pressure plates) or maybe even a table (again, equally easily made using a fence and pressure plates). You'll find out how to build these items in the "Building machines for your rooms" section, later in this chapter.

If the empty space is outside, add a garden or a farm. A garden makes a building look nicer. A farm is an excellent way to get food and other material, and having it close to your building is handy. But, if you want a quiet area around your building, a farm probably isn't the way to go, because the animals are noisy. For more information on farms, look to Chapter 8. To learn how to build a garden, look back to Chapter 10.

If you want something a little less ordinary, use the empty space to build something cool and creative such as a secret room. In Minecraft, you can build anything you want, so why not use this opportunity to build something awesome?

Adding decorative flourishes

Furniture and paintings work well when you need for your room to look more comfortable and home-like. You have lots of choices for the types of furniture you can make, from lamps to coffee tables to bunk beds. Just remember that when you create furniture, you're creating items that are decorative rather than practical. If you were to make a chair, for example, it would be a nice-looking chair, but you wouldn't be able to sit in it.

Signs

To see how this decorative thing could work, start out by making a sign. Follow these steps:

1. **Break (left click) a tree to produce 2 wood blocks.**

2. **Place the 2 wood blocks on the crafting table, and exchange them for the 8 wooden planks that appear.**

3. **Create 4 sticks by placing 2 of the wooden planks in the middle column of the crafting table, using the lower and middle box, as shown in Figure 6-1.**

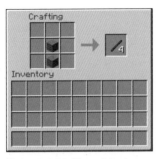

Figure 6-1: Making sticks from wooden planks.

4. Take the sticks and place them in your inventory.

5. Place the remaining 6 wooden planks on the crafting table, filling the top two rows.

6. In the middle box on the bottom, place 1 stick.

7. Take the three signs in exchange for the planks and stick.

Congratulations! You have successfully made a sign. A sign is for decoration, but it's not useless. You can write on signs and hang them where you please. To do this, just place the sign where you want it. A magnified version of the sign should come up on the screen. Then use the keyboard to write whatever you want.

Stairs

Another piece of furniture is the wooden stairs. They're useful because they act as stairs (both practical and decorative), can make roofing look better, and can act as the seat of a chair. To make wooden stairs, all you need is 6 wooden planks. After you have those, go into the crafting table and place 3 of the planks on the bottom row. Then, place 2 planks in the middle and right boxes of the middle column. Lastly, place 1 plank on the top row's right box. They should look like stairs in the boxes of the craft table. Then take the wooden stairs in exchange for the planks.

Chairs

After you've become an expert at making a sign and wooden stairs, you have all the skills you need to make a great chair! Not only is it simple, but it also looks great in a room. To create a chair, place a wooden stair where you want the chair to be, then place two signs on either side of the stair. That's it; instant chair! For an example of a chair, check out Figure 6-2.

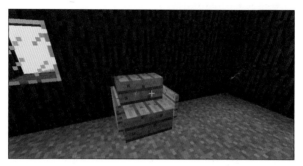

Figure 6-2: A chair in Minecraft.

Paintings

A painting is a useful way to make your room look pleasant. To make a painting, you need 8 sticks and 1 piece of wool. Place the wool in the middle box of the crafting table, and then place the sticks in the remaining boxes surrounding the wool. Take the painting in exchange for the wool and sticks. You can place (right click) the painting anywhere you like on a wall; however, you cannot choose how big the painting will be nor the subject of the painting. There are 26 paintings that can appear, most of them depicting people or places.

Building machines for your rooms

Machines can not only help you survive and defend your building but also help lighten up a room. A furnace cooks your food and makes it edible, smelts various minerals into ingots, and can even serve as a light. Given all the things a furnace can do for you, you'd be foolish *not* to furnish one of your rooms with a furnace.

Here's the drill: To make a furnace, you need 8 pieces of cobblestone. To get cobblestone, just mine stone that can be found underground. Place the cobblestone in the outside boxes of the crafting table, leaving the center box empty. Then take the furnace in exchange for the cobblestone. Wood, wood planks, coal, blocks of coal, charcoal, blaze rods, and lava buckets can power a furnace.

Chests, crafting tables, bookshelves, sticks, saplings, jukeboxes, note blocks, locked chests, wooden pressure plates, wooden stairs, trapdoors, and fences also serve as fuels. However, they are less efficient.

A furnace is important, but it's also quite basic. Something a little more difficult is an arrow-shooting dispenser. This awesome machine is great for defending your building.

The way the dispenser works is that redstone gives the dispenser power. Redstone is an ore that can be mined into redstone dust; the dust is what powers the dispenser. The dispenser then shoots out its contents, so when you power it up and place an arrow inside, it becomes an arrow-shooting dispenser. It's a wonderful addition to a castle or the surrounding wall of a village.

To build an arrow-shooting dispenser, you need 7 cobblestones, 1 bow, as many arrows as you can make, a redstone torch, and at least 2 units of redstone dust.

To get cobblestone, mine stone and pick up the cobblestone that drops when you're finished. To create one bow, you need 3 strings and 3 sticks. (You can get string from killing a skeleton or cave spider.) Place the strings in the right column of the crafting table, filling all the boxes. Then, place 2 of the sticks in the top and bottom boxes of the middle column. Now, place the last stick in the center box of the left column.

To make arrows, you need a flint, a stick, and a feather. Mine gravel to get flint, and kill a chicken to get feathers. Place the flint in the top box of the center column, and the stick in the box below it. Then, place the feather in the bottom box.

You'll need a redstone torch to activate your dispenser. To make one, you need 1 redstone dust and 1 stick. (Redstone dust is dropped when mining redstone ore.) Place the stick in the lower box of the middle column in the crafting table; place the redstone powder in the box above it.

Redstone dust is extremely important when building this kind of dispenser, because without it, your dispenser wouldn't work!

Now, you need to build the dispenser. To do that, you need 7 cobblestones, the bow, and redstone dust. Here's what to do with them:

1. **Place the bow in the middle box of the crafting table.**

2. **Place 1 unit of redstone dust in the lower middle box of the crafting table.**

3. **Place the 7 cobblestones in the remaining boxes.**

4. **Exchange the redstone powder, the bow, and the cobblestone for the dispenser.**

Now your dispenser is ready. You can place it anywhere in the building. If you want to kill zombies and other enemies when the sun goes down, place the dispenser at eye level and outside. If you place it too high, the arrows don't hit anything.

To use the arrow-shooting dispenser, follow these steps:

1. **Place the arrows inside the dispenser.**

   To do this, just right click the dispenser and place the arrows into one of the boxes of the dispenser. It doesn't matter which box you use.

2. **Place the redstone dust in a line until you reach the spot where you want to stand when you turn on the dispenser.**

3. **Set a red torch next to the end of the redstone dust trail.**

   This step turns on the dispenser so that it shoots arrows. If you want to turn off the dispenser, just destroy the torch.

Another useful machine is a locking iron door. Iron doors are useful because they're extremely hard to break. You make it out of 6 iron ingots and open it using a lever or button.

Follow these steps to make a locking iron door:

1. **Place the ingots on the crafting table.**

   The bars should fill the left and middle columns of the table. An iron door appears.

2. **Take the iron door in exchange for the bars.**

3. **Place the door where you want it, and place at least 2 vertical blocks next to the door (just one side is fine).**

   You do this so that you can place a lever or button on the block to open the door.

4. **Get a piece of wooden plank or a piece of stone to make a button.**

5. **Place the stone or plank on the middle block of the crafting table.**

6. **Take the button in exchange for the planks or stone.**

7. **Place the button on a block next to the door.**

   You now have a functioning steel door that you can open with the press of a button!

When you use a button to open a steel door, it closes after two or three seconds.

Another way to open an iron door is with a lever. To create a lever, you need 1 block of cobblestone and a stick. Making a lever is easy — follow these steps:

1. **Place the cobblestone in the lower middle box of the crafting table.**

2. **Place the stick in the center box of the crafting table.**

3. **Take the lever in exchange for the cobblestone and the stick.**

4. **Place the lever on the block next to the door.**

You can use the lever by right clicking it. The door will stay open until you manually shut it. After you open the door, place a second lever or button on the other side. The first lever opens the door, while the second lever closes it.

Wait, there's more! You can also use a pressure plate to open an iron door. A *pressure plate,* like the name implies, is a plate that opens a door (among other things) when you put pressure on it. To make one, you need 2 stones or woods.

To make a pressure plate, follow these instructions:

1. **Place 2 wooden planks or 2 stone in the middle row's left and middle boxes of the crafting table.**

2. **Take the pressure plate in exchange for the planks or stones, and place it on the ground in front of the door.**

3. **Walk on the pressure plate to open the door.**

   The door will close on its own.

A pressure plate is often used to make traps. For example, if you wire TNT to a pressure plate, another player or mob will explode when walking over the plate.

A wooden pressure plate can be triggered by dropped items; an iron plate cannot.

7

Using Block Textures

*M*inecraft has lots of different types of blocks, and each type of block has its own texture. Texture usually refers to how something *feels,* but in Minecraft you can't really feel a block because, well, it's online. Instead, you can get an idea of what a block would feel like based on how the block *looks.* For example, cobblestone looks like it would feel rough because it looks like it has grooves in it. An iron block looks smooth because it's completely flat on all sides.

Each type of block and texture gives a building a certain look or feel — like a personality. By the end of this chapter, you should have a feel for which types of blocks you want to use for different structures.

Using Smooth Textures

Blocks with a smooth texture look flat on all sides. You can use these blocks to make a building look clean or even fancy. A few types of smooth blocks are wooden planks, blocks of gold, or blocks of diamond — all are excellent blocks for buildings. Figure 7-1 shows the basic smooth textures in Minecraft.

Figure 7-1: Smooth block textures in Minecraft.

You can make many different types of smooth blocks. A common choice involves using wooden planks, but you have to look at Chapter 6 to find out about them. In this chapter, we show you how to make blocks of iron, diamond, gold, lapis lazuli, emerald, quartz, or redstone. To make any of these block types, follow these steps:

1. **Mine 9 of the required ore with a pickaxe.**

   The ore can be iron, gold, diamond, lapis lazuli, emerald, quartz, or redstone. Mining the ore gives you blocks of the ore, but they aren't quite smooth, so you have to make them into gems (see Step 2).

2. **Smelt the 9 ore blocks in the furnace.**

   When an ore block is smelted, it becomes a gem.

3. **Place the resulting 9 gems into the crafting table, filling all the boxes.**

4. **Take the block that appears in exchange for the gems.**

When you use smooth blocks for a building, it can truly turn heads. Smooth blocks work well for building classy structures such as museums. Figure 7-2 shows an example of a house using only smooth blocks (in this case, wooden planks and lapis lazuli blocks).

Figure 7-2: A smooth house.

You can also use smooth textures to make rough textures stand out. When you put smooth and rough textures together, they contrast with each other in a good way. (We talk about rough textures and how to use them with smooth textures later in this chapter.)

Using Rough Block Textures

Rough block textures look cracked with sort of a 3D effect on the outside. For example, both netherrack and cobblestone are rough textures because their surfaces look rough and broken. Figure 7-3 shows the basic rough block textures.

You'll find that rough-textured blocks are quite versatile — you can use different rough textures to give buildings different impressions. For example, if you want a building to look old and rustic, rough-texture blocks (such as cobblestone) are good choices.

You can also use rough-textured blocks to make smooth-textured blocks stand out. For example, if you used only wooden planks for a building but then placed a netherrack as a trim, the wooden planks would stand out. Figure 7-4 shows a house using only rough textures.

Figure 7-3: Rough block textures in Minecraft.

Figure 7-4: A house made of rough textures.

Creating an Older-Looking Structure

Creating an older-looking structure is a lot of fun. First, you need to decide what type of blocks you want to use. For an old or abandoned building, rough blocks usually look best. Rough blocks such as cobblestone, netherrack, and obsidian (see Chapter 4) are all good choices. Here are the instructions for building a structure that looks old:

1. **Make a floor plan.**

   Simply think about the size of your building. Do you want it big or small?

2. **Make a wireframe of your building (see Chapter 5) and fill it in.**

   A *wireframe* is a block outline of a structure in the game. You fill in the wall by placing blocks inside your wireframe to create a wall.

3. **Place your decorations.**

Building an older-looking structure is just like building a regular structure, except for the decorations. The next few sections tell you exactly how to make your structure look old and abandoned.

Cracked blocks

Cracked blocks such as cobblestone and obsidian are useful for adding age to a building. They help set the mood of an abandoned building. You can also use other cracked blocks such as cracked stone brick, netherrack, bedrock, and bricks.

You can use rough blocks as cracked walls or paths. If you're not sure how to build a wall, flip over to Chapter 4. To build a path, follow these steps:

1. **Dig a series of holes where you want the path to be.**

   You need the hole to be only 1 block deep, but it can go deeper.

2. **Gather the blocks to fill the holes you just dug.**

   The blocks should have a rough texture. They don't have to be the same as the blocks you used to build the walls, but they should be rough.

3. **Place rough blocks into each hole until the path is finished.**

For an example of walls and paths made by cracked blocks, look at Figure 7-5.

Figure 7-5: Use cracked blocks to make your building look old or abandoned.

Mossy blocks

Mossy blocks are helpful for decorating and building abandoned structures — they make buildings look truly old and forgotten. Minecraft offers a few types of mossy blocks: mossy stone block, mossy stone bricks, and mossy cobblestone wall. The mossy stone block is the most basic kind of mossy block; you use it to make the other types of mossy blocks. Mossy stone bricks are simply bricks that look mossy. Mossy cobblestone is similar to mossy stone brick, but it looks like cobblestone.

To make 1 mossy cobblestone block, follow these steps:

1. **Gather 1 block of cobblestone by breaking regular stone blocks.**

   Stone is extremely easy to find: Just dig down until you find it.

   To break a block, left-click and hold down until the block breaks.

2. **Use a shear to get 1 vine from a tree in a jungle or swamp.**

   To make a shear, you need 2 iron ingots. Place them both in the crafting table, with one in the bottom box of the left column and the other in the center box. Take the shear in exchange for the iron ingots.

   When you find a tree with vines growing on it, use a shear to break off the vine; it will fall to the ground. Walk over the fallen vine to pick it up.

3. **Place the cobblestone in the middle box in the left column of the crafting table, and place the vine in the center box.**

4. **Take the 6 mossy cobblestone blocks that appear in exchange for the cobblestone and vine.**

Mossy cobblestone can also be found in Mega Taiga biomes. Also, mossy stone bricks can be found in strongholds.

Now that you know how to make a mossy cobblestone, you can make a mossy cobblestone wall. Follow these steps:

1. **Make 6 mossy cobblestone blocks out of regular cobblestone and vines (see the preceding step list).**

2. **Place the 6 mossy cobblestone blocks on the crafting table, filling the lower two rows (see Figure 7-6).**

Figure 7-6: Making a mossy cobblestone wall.

3. **Take the mossy cobblestone wall in exchange for the mossy cobblestone. Repeat until you have the amount of walls you need.**

Making mossy stone bricks is a little more complicated than making mossy cobblestone blocks.

1. **Gather 4 stones and place them on the crafting table.**

   Place 1 stone in the lower left corner, 1 in the middle box of the left column, 1 in the center box, and 1 in the lower box of the center column. See Figure 7-7 for an example.

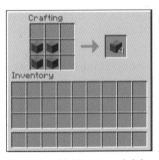

Figure 7-7: Making stone bricks.

2. **Take the stone bricks in exchange for the stone.**

3. **Travel to a Jungle or Swamp biome.**

4. **Walk up to a tree that has a vine growing on it, and use shears to break the vine.**

5. **Walk over the vine to pick it up.**

6. **Place the vine and stone on the crafting table.**

   The stone goes into the middle box of the left column, and the vine goes into the center box.

7. **Take the mossy stone brick in exchange for the stone brick and vine.**

Now that you know how to make mossy cobblestone blocks, mossy cobblestone walls, and mossy stone bricks, you can add all these items to the aged structure, to make it look even older. Figure 7-8 shows an abandoned structure using all these elements.

Figure 7-8: An abandoned structure with mossy elements.

Damaged walls

Damaged walls contribute to the effect of an older-looking structure, too — and you don't even have to gather materials to make them. All you need is a wall!

To get started, just go to a wall and start destroying random blocks. You don't need to stick to a pattern when you're destroying blocks — tear up whatever you think looks right.

Destroying a wall might seem counterproductive at first, but don't worry — the result is extremely cool. Check out Figure 7-9 if you don't believe us. Decaying walls make a building look like it hasn't been taken care of in a while and adds to its overall tone — the tone of an older-looking structure.

Figure 7-9: A structure using damaged walls.

Vines

Vines are not only decorative but also useful. When vines grow down the structure, you can use them for climbing and hiding from mobs. We tell you more about those scenarios in a minute. First, though, you need to start some vines growing. Here's how to do it:

1. **Travel to a Jungle or Swamp biome and find a tree with vines growing on it.**

2. **Using a shear, break off as many vines as you want and pick them up.**

3. **Travel back to your building and place the vines on the side of the roof, as shown in Figure 7-10.**

Figure 7-10: A vine placed on the side of the building.

4. Wait for the vine to grow down the side of your building.

If you don't want to wait for the vine to grow down, you can place more vines below it to make it look like it grew down.

Figure 7-11 shows an abandoned structure with vines.

Now that you have vines growing down your structure, let's talk about how useful they are for climbing and hiding.

When you put a solid block next to a vine, you can climb up and down the vine as though it's a ladder. If there isn't a solid block next to the vine, you only climb down the vine, not up.

Figure 7-11: A structure using vines.

Vines also help you hide from mobs. Vines block the mobs' line of sight, so you can hide behind them if you're in trouble at night. As a bonus, you can shoot arrows through vines, though a skeleton's arrow won't make it through.

Cobwebs

Cobwebs are similar to vines, in that both are for decoration but are also useful. You can't make cobwebs; you have to find them, destroy them, and pick them up. You can find cobwebs in dungeons or abandoned mineshafts.

To destroy cobwebs, you have to use shears with the Silk Touch enchantment. You can get this enchantment in two ways: Create a book that you then enchant with the Silk Touch enchantment or find a book in a dungeon that's already been enchanted with Silk Touch.

If you plan to create a book empowered with Silk Touch, you should know that it may take a long time. The process requires making a book, gathering obsidian and diamond blocks, and then enchanting the book. The catch is that you can't simply choose the Silk Touch enchantment — book enchantments are random. If you don't get silk touch on the first try, you have to keep trying until you persevere.

To make an enchanted book, you need a regular book and an enchantment table. Keep reading to find out how to make both.

Making a regular book

You can't enchant something you don't have, right? So you need to make a book that you can add an enchantment to. To make a regular book, follow these steps:

1. **Gather three sugar canes from a sugar cane plant.**

   A full-grown sugar cane plant will give you three sugar canes.

   To break sugar cane, click and hold until it breaks. Then, walk over it to pick it up.

2. **Place the sugar canes on the crafting table.**

   You'll want to put the first sugar cane into the middle box of the left column, the next one in the center box, and the last one in the middle box of the right column.

3. **Take the three paper you receive in exchange for the sugar canes.**

4. **Find and butcher a cow for its leather.**

   To butcher a cow, click on it until it dies.

5. **Walk over the leather to pick it up.**

6. **Place the paper and leather on the crafting table to make a book.**

   Place 2 paper in the middle column, filling the top two boxes. Place the last paper in the middle box of the left column. Place the leather in the bottom box of the middle column, as shown in Figure 7-12.

7. **Take the book in exchange for the leather and the paper.**

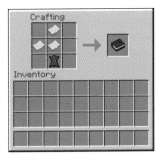

Figure 7-12: How to make a book.

Making an enchantment table

Enchantments need a tad more than your standard crafting table — in fact, they need an honest-to-goodness enchantment table. To create one, you need to mine 2 diamonds and 4 obsidian with a pickaxe (see Chapter 4). You also need to create 1 book, but you should already be set if you've worked through the preceding section.

Mining obsidian and diamond can be difficult because of how rare they are. You can mine diamond only with iron or diamond pickaxes, and you can mine obsidian only with a diamond pickaxe.

Even though obsidian is rare, you can get it in a few ways: Mine it or create it. Mining obsidian requires a diamond pickaxe and lots of time. Creating obsidian is much easier, but after you create it, you have to mine it with a diamond pickaxe.

Here's how to create obsidian:

1. **Make a bucket using 3 iron ingots.**

   Place 1 ingot in the middle box of the left column of the crafting table. Place the next ingot in the bottom box of the center column, and place the last one in the middle box of the right column.

2. **Take the bucket in exchange for the iron ingots.**

3. **Travel to a Beach biome.**

4. **Using the bucket, scoop up water (right-click to scoop).**

5. **Place the water where you want the obsidian to be.**

   Don't overthink where to put the water. The location doesn't matter because you're going to mine the obsidian anyway.

6. **Take the now empty bucket and find lava, either aboveground or below it.**

   If you plan to find lava aboveground, wait until nighttime. At night, lava is easier to see because of the light it gives off. If you plan to find lava belowground, start digging by breaking blocks (click and hold until the block breaks).

7. **Right-click to scoop the lava into your bucket.**

8. **Place the lava where the full block of water is by right-clicking the mouse.**

   A full block of water will take up one block. If you do not place the lava on a full block, then you will get cobblestone instead of obsidian.

   Mixing water and lava makes obsidian.

Now that you've made (or found) obsidian, mine it with a diamond pickaxe. (See Chapter 4 for more information on pickaxes.) You need 4 obsidian to make the enchantment table, so make sure that you mine a sufficient amount.

You also need 2 diamonds. Diamonds are rare and extremely valuable. Mining 2 diamonds might take a while, but it's worth every second. To mine, you only need a pickaxe and some torches. First, dig down into the ground until you find any type of resource, such as coal or iron. That's a sign that you're getting close. Then just keep digging until you find diamond ore. (For more on mining, check out Chapter 4.)

At this point, you have a book and some obsidian and diamonds — everything you need to make an enchantment table. To make the enchantment table, follow these steps:

1. **Right-click to open the crafting table.**

2. **Place three obsidian into each box of the bottom row and one in the center box.**

3. **Place one diamond in the middle box of the left column, and the other in the middle box of the right column.**

4. **Place the book in the top box of the middle column.**

5. **Take the enchanting table in exchange for the obsidian, book, and diamond.**

Enchanting a book

Now that you have an enchanting table, you can use it to enchant a book!

1. **Make 1 book to use in the enchanting table.**

2. **Open the enchantment table and place the book in the box on the left, as shown in Figure 7-13.**

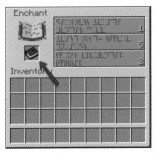

Figure 7-13: Make sure your book is in the right box.

3. **Click on one of the tan rectangular boxes that pop up on the right (see Figure 7-14).**

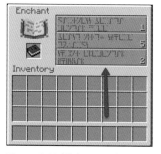

Figure 7-14: Pick an enchantment for your book.

4. **Drag your mouse over the now enchanted book.**

This step is optional, but by doing this, you activate a pop-up box that tells you what particular enchantment you managed to get. Figure 7-15 shows you an example of an enchanted book.

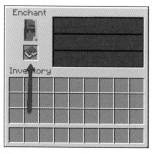

Figure 7-15: You finally have an enchanted book!

Rarely do you get a Silk Touch book on the first try. You'll more likely get another kind of enchantment — and then have to repeat the whole enchantment process until you have enchanted a book with Silk Touch.

Finding a dungeon

If you're not in the mood to put much effort into creating your own Silk Touch book, there's another way you can get one: dungeons. A dungeon is a small, underground room made of mossy cobblestone. Inside this room, there is a monster spawner, and usually a chest (and sometimes two!).

Finding Silk Touch books in dungeons takes time and persistence (but probably not as much time and persistence as making your own). To find an enchanted book in a dungeon, follow these steps:

1. **Make a pickaxe (see Chapter 4) and start digging.**

   Dungeons are underground and you're trying to find one. There's no way to know whether you're above a dungeon, but they're pretty big, so you will most likely find one.

2. **When you find a dungeon, start looking for a chest.**

3. **When you find a chest, open it.**

   A chest in a dungeon usually contains rare or random objects. What you want to find is a chest with a Silk Touch enchanted book.

   If the chest doesn't have the book, see if there's a second chest and try that one. If you have no luck there, then it's time to then start searching for a different dungeon.

Making an anvil

When you've finally found a Silk Touch enchanted book (whether you made it or found it), you need to make an anvil so that you can enchant your shears. To make an anvil, you need 31 iron ingots and these instructions:

1. **Open the crafting table.**

2. **Place 9 of the iron ingots into the crafting table, filling every box.**

3. **Take the block of iron in exchange for the iron ingots.**

4. **Repeat Steps 2 and 3 until you have 3 blocks of iron.**

5. **Place the 3 blocks of iron in the top row of the crafting table.**

6. **Place 3 iron ingots in the bottom row of the crafting table.**

7. **Place the last iron ingot into the center box of the crafting table.**

8. **Take the anvil in exchange for the iron blocks and ingots.**

Enchanting shears

Finally! It's time to make some Silk Touch enchanted shears. Open the anvil, place your shear in the first box, and place the Silk Touch enchanted book in the second box, as shown in Figure 7-16. Then just take the enchanted shears that appear in the last box, and you're done!

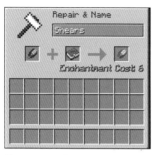

Figure 7-16: How to make an enchanted shear.

Now go get those cobwebs — you've earned them!

The best places to find cobwebs are in dungeons and abandoned mineshafts.

Block Textures That Work Well Together

Some block textures look good together, and others simply don't. For example, most smooth and rough textured blocks look good together because they contrast and make each other stand out. Too much of one texture, however, doesn't look good.

Finding block textures that look good together has a lot to do with not only texture but also color. Before you decide what texture you want for your building, decide what color you want. After you know what color you want, look at blocks having that color. Choose the texture that fits well with the other blocks that will surround that block.

8

Farming

In This Chapter

▶ Building your own farm

▶ Planting crops

▶ Breeding animals

*M*inecraft must have a green thumb, because it makes farming — both crop farming and animal farming — an easy undertaking. This chapter shows you just how easy.

Preparing the Land for Your Farm

Not only is farming easy, but it also provides an abundant amount of food — from plants as well as animals. But you can't just dive in and start planting seeds and herding animals. Nope. Just like in the real world, the first thing you have to do is prepare the land. In Minecraft, that means you need three things: a hoe, fence blocks, and land.

To make a hoe, follow these steps:

1. Gather 2 wooden planks and 2 sticks.

You make sticks by placing 2 wooden planks into the crafting table, filling the middle column's bottom 2 boxes.

2. Open the crafting table.

3. Place the wooden planks in the top middle and top right boxes; place the sticks in the center box and the box below it.

4. Take the hoe in exchange for the planks and sticks.

To build a wooden fence, follow these steps:

1. Gather 6 sticks.

2. Place the sticks in the bottom two rows of the crafting table.

3. Take the 2 fences in exchange for the sticks.

You need only 1 hoe, but the number of wooden fences you need depends on the size of your farm. Your farm doesn't have to be any specific size — you can have a small farm that's easy to manage or a large farm that is a little more difficult.

After you have your tools, you can't use them until you find land to farm! Try to find land that is as flat as possible and is made of dirt or grass blocks. Sand is okay, but you can't plant many crops in it.

Part of preparing your land involves placing fencing, creating a water source, and fertilizing the dirt or grass so that you can plant seeds. When you have your land picked out, follow these instructions to prepare it:

1. Build a fence around your farm, using the fences you built earlier.

2. Dig out a series of rows, 1 block apart, that extend the length of your fenced-in area, as shown in Figure 8-1.

   These rows will be your water source so that your crops can grow.

Figure 8-1: Making irrigation ditches for the water.

3. Create a bucket.

You make a bucket by smelting iron ore in a furnace to make ingots and then placing 3 ingots in the crafting table: 1 in the bottom box of the middle column, 1 in the left box of the middle row, and 1 in the right box of the middle row, as shown in Figure 8-2.

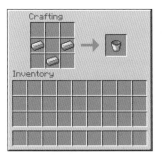

Figure 8-2: How to make a bucket.

4. Travel to a beach and walk up to the water's edge.

5. Right-click to scoop up water with your bucket.

6. Walk back to your farm and fill the holes with the water.

Depending on the size of your farm, it might take you a few trips to retrieve enough water to fill all the holes.

7. Use the hoe on the remaining dirt or grass blocks.

Hoeing the grass makes the grass or dirt block fertilized. You have to fertilize your land before you can plant any crops.

Using bone meal on crops makes them grow faster. To get bone meal, place 1 bone from a killed skeleton into the crafting table. *Note:* When used on a pumpkin, bone meal makes the stem of the pumpkin fully mature, but the pumpkin itself doesn't appear immediately.

Whew! Tired? Good thing it was your Minecraft character and not you doing all that hard work, because you're not done yet. You still need to plant crops.

Reaping What You Sow

You might be wondering what crop to plant, and how many of those crops you'll need. To figure this out, just think about your goal. Look at Table 8-1 for help. When you know what seed you want to use, place 1 seed into 1 block of fertilized soil.

Table 8-1	Types of Crops and Their Uses			
Crop	**Where to Get Seed**	**Type of Block to Plant On**	**When to Harvest**	**Uses**
Wheat	Break long grass.	Fertile farmland	When the tips of the wheat are golden	To make hay and food items
Melon	Break and obtain melon found in Jungle biomes.	Fertile farmland	When melon appears next to the melon stem	Food source and potion item
Pumpkin	Craft pumpkin blocks into pumpkin seed.	Fertile farmland	When pumpkin appears next to pumpkin stem	Can make pie, helmets, and golems

Crop	Where to Get Seed	Type of Block to Plant On	When to Harvest	Uses
Sugar cane	Plant sugar cane item instead of seed.	Grass, dirt, sand, or red sand	When 3 blocks high	Paper and sugar
Carrot	Plant carrot item instead of seed.	Fertile farmland	When you can see carrot appearing near ground.	Food source; can be used to make golden carrot — a food source that also heals, grows, and tames horses and donkeys
Potato	Plant potato item instead of seed.	Fertile farmland	When you can see a potato emerging from the ground	As a food source
Cacti	Plant cacti item instead of seed.	Sand	When 3 blocks high	To make green dye

Two crop seeds — cocoa beans and the mysterious nether wart — are a tad less common, but each has its own, special appeal.

Cocoa beans are cool because you can use them to make cookies, and everyone likes cookies. You can also use cocoa beans to make brown dye, but that's not as popular as cookies. To find cocoa beans, you have to venture into the jungle and track down a cocoa tree — look for tall green trees with vines growing down them. You can plant and harvest the beans on the trunks of the jungle trees.

The color of the cocoa beans tells you whether they're ready to harvest yet:

- **Orange beans are ripe and ready.** When you break an orange pod, you get 2 cocoa beans.

- **Yellow beans aren't quite ripe.** If you break a yellow pod, you get only 2 beans.

- **Green beans aren't ready.** When you break a green pod, you get only 1 bean.

To make cookies and brown dye, you need only 1 cocoa bean for each.

Nether wart is often used in potions (like the awkward potion), which is cool, but nether wart is a difficult plant to find. To get nether wart seeds, you have to use a portal to travel from the overworld (where you are now) into the Nether. When you reach the Nether, start exploring until you find a nether fortress. Then, start exploring that fortress until you find nether wart — it's a deep red and looks a bit like a lollipop that grows out of soul sand.

Follow these steps to gather nether wart seeds:

1. **Left-click to break the nether wart.**

2. **Left-click to break the block it was growing from.**

   You need that block, known as soul sand, to plant nether wart. Soul sand is a little different from regular sand and soil because you don't need a hoe to make it fertile.

3. **Walk over the 2 items to pick them up.**

After you've gathered the nether wart and soul sand, you can return to the overworld through the portal you made earlier.

When you return to your farm, dig a hole in the ground and place the soul sand in the hole, and then plant the nether wart in the sand.

Alrighty then. The land is prepped, and the crops are planted — the only thing left to do is wait until the crops are grown and ready to harvest. Figure 8-3 shows you what one of our farms looks like when the crops are grown.

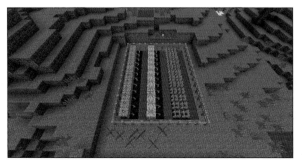

Figure 8-3: A finished farm.

Wait until the crops have grown out of the ground and are tall before harvesting.

After a crop is grown, you can harvest it by clicking on the crop to break it. Walk over it to pick it up, and it's automatically stored in the inventory. For the specific harvest information for each crop and when to harvest, refer to Table 8-1.

Animal Farming

Animals are a good resource to have because you can use them for a food source or to harvest things they produce, such as eggs and wool. For animal farming, you don't need any type of special land. Most people make a farm near their house or base, but the placement is completely up to you.

Before you gather your animals, you need to make a pen for them. Create separate pens for each type of animal — for example, cows in one pen and sheep in another. To make a pen, create as many wooden fences as you need to make the pen the size you want. After you have the fences, place (right click) the fences in a square or rectangular shape. This is the pen that will hold your animals.

Breeding animals

Breeding animals gives you a reliable food source as well as a number of raw materials that could come in very handy.

To breed animals, you have to lure two of the same kind into your pen. You can do that by holding food they like so that they'll follow you — Table 8-2 has more information on what kind of food works for which animal.

If food isn't an option, you can use a *lead*, which is sort of like a leash. You loop it around an animal's neck and lead them into a pen. To make a lead, you need 4 strings and a slime ball. You can get string by killing regular spiders or cave spiders. To get a slimeball, you have to kill a slime. There's no special way to kill spiders and slimes; just hit them until they die.

To make a lead, place a slimeball in the center box of the crafting table. Place 1 string in the left column's top two boxes, the third string in the second column's top box, and the last string in the right column's last box. Figure 8-4 shows how to make a lead. To actually *use* a lead, right click an animal while holding the lead.

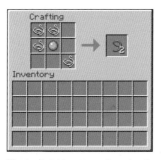

Figure 8-4: How to make a lead.

When you get the animals into the pen, bring them near each other. Then feed both of them food they like. (Again, Table 8-2 gives you some ideas.)

Table 8-2	Farming Animals	
Animal	**Feed**	**Used For**
Chicken	Seeds of wheat, melon, pumpkin, or nether wart	Eggs, feathers, chicken (meat)
Cow	Wheat	Beef, leather, milk
Mushroom cow	Wheat	Milk, beef, mushrooms

Animal	Feed	Used For
Sheep	Wheat	Wool
Pig	Carrots	Pork chops
Tamed wolf (dog)	Chicken, beef, pork chop, or rotten flesh	Companion
Tamed ocelot (cat)	Fish	Companion
Horse	Golden carrot or apple	Transportation

When taming a wolf, the meat can be either raw or cooked. When taming an ocelot, the fish needs to be raw.

With both animals in the pen, hold out the food they like and use it to lure one animal toward the other. When they're close to each other, feed the food to one of the animals until it has hearts around it, and then do the same thing with the other animal. After a few seconds, a smaller version of the animals appears next to them. You can continue breeding until you have as many animals as you want.

Figure 8-5: A baby animal.

You don't have to keep dogs and cats in a pen in order to breed them.

Using animal as resources

Just about every animal produces a resource you can use. For example, chickens produce eggs, sheep provide wool, and cows give milk.

You pick up a resource by walking over it. Any resources you pick up are automatically stored in your inventory.

Animal farms are especially helpful when you're in Survival mode, because you have a food source near you and you don't have to go hunting.

Pigs offer fairly limited resources — they only drop pork chops when butchered.

Cows, on the other hand, are particularly good resources. You can milk them indefinitely (hold a bucket, and then right-click the cow), or you can butcher them to get raw beef and leather. To butcher a cow, just keep hitting it until it dies.

A *mushroom cow* is almost exactly the same as a regular cow; it just looks like a red and white mushroom! They also have mushrooms growing on their backs. When the mushroom cows are sheared, they turn into regular cows and drop 5 mushrooms.

Leather is a good resource because you can use it to make a variety of things, including armor. (But you should know that when you butcher a cow, it doesn't always drop leather.)

Chickens are popular because they frequently drop eggs that you can pick up — just walk over them. You can butcher a chicken to get meat and feathers. Figure 8-6 shows a working animal farm.

Figure 8-6: A working animal farm.

9

Using Advanced Building Techniques

In This Chapter

▶ Adding randomness to your world

▶ Going polygonal

▶ Working with circles and spheres

▶ Getting your world wet

*I*n addition to the general advice we give you throughout this book, we share several neat tricks to help you build the world of your dreams. This chapter shows you how to use some of these tricks to create all sorts of cool-looking structures and textures.

Using Randomized Block Patterns

Patterns have a big impact on your designs, decorations, and buildings. For example, it's easy to use simple patterns to create a sense of order. Of course, the world rarely follows simple patterns. Can you imagine what it would look like if everything were the same shape? Borrrrring.

Sometimes you want a structure to look more natural, chaotic, or realistic — this is where random patterns enter the picture. Many designs, especially those meant to re-create natural structures such as forests or caverns, have blocks placed all over to make things look more authentic. Think about it: When you're in the country, do you see trees scattered around or all lined up? Unless you're looking at an orchard, it's a good bet that they're scattered.

Applying randomness to surfaces

To see what a difference a little randomness can make, take a look at Figure 9-1. The figure shows two walls made of stone and gravel. The one on the left has a consistent checkerboard pattern, and the one on the right has a random and sporadic pattern. The random pattern makes the wall on the right look gritty and timeworn — just what you'd think a stone-and-gravel wall would look like.

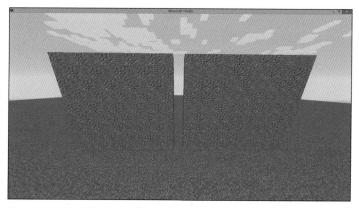

Figure 9-1: Using blocks randomly to create an engaging tone.

Similarly, Figure 9-2 shows another application of random block patterns. This wall is made of stone bricks, but it also has a few mossy and cracked bricks spaced throughout. By breaking up a generic surface with a few different (but similar) blocks, you can make your structure look more real.

Random block patterns generally work best with big surfaces. If you're not sure whether you should use a random pattern, just try it out and see how it looks — you can always change it later.

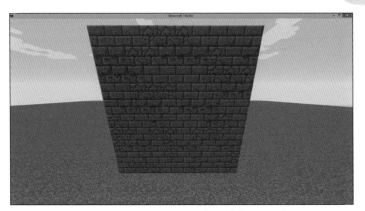

Figure 9-2: Placing a few random blocks around a structure.

Applying randomness to landscaping

Sometimes you want to build some small, natural-looking areas. In those cases, definitely use a bit of randomness so that the areas look more realistic. Suppose that you want to make a little grassy hill for a zoo or a centerpiece decoration. A pyramid, or a dome, or any sort of hill that looks obviously manmade would ruin the effect.

To get the natural look you're going for, follow these steps:

1. **Build the bottom layer of the landscape.**

   Come up with a random flat shape, and build it — the rest of the landscape should be built on top of it.

2. **Reshape the layer until it's in the shape you want.**

   Work out any flat or misshapen parts that don't seem compatible with the rest of the shape. For example, if something seems too flat or jagged, take away blocks to make it resemble a shape closer to what you are picturing.

3. **Build a second layer on top of the first.**

   Create another random flat shape. If you're making a hill or mountain, the second layer should be a slightly smaller than the first. Remember that a single shape might turn into multiple shapes at higher layers.

4. **Reshape the second layer.**

   Make sure that the first layer transitions smoothly into the second.

5. **Keep adding layers until the landscape is completed.**

   The smaller each layer is than the last, the shorter the landscape will be.

You can follow these steps to construct almost any landscape. If you want to create a cave, go underground and dig out the walls and ceiling layer by layer. If you want to construct a hill with multiple types of blocks (such as dirt on top of sand on top of stone), just complete the preceding steps for each type of block.

Constructing Polygons for Your Structures

Most basic buildings have rectangular foundations — a simple one-room structure usually looks like some sort of box. But you want to think *outside* the box, right? Yeah, we thought you were the creative type. In this section, we tell you how you can use different *polygons* (shapes composed of straight lines) to make some truly awesome rooms.

Building slanted walls

In Minecraft, walls are generally straight because, when you're building with cubes, you usually place them side by side and on top of one another. But that doesn't mean that all walls have to be straight — you can construct slanted walls, too.

Figure 9-3 shows three examples of slanted walls. All three are working walls (no entity can pass through them), and they all have a similar design (steps). The wall on the left is composed of single blocks along a diagonal. The walls in the middle and right are the same, except that rather than single blocks, they're composed of 2-block and 3-block segments, respectively. This allows you to build steeper and steeper slants.

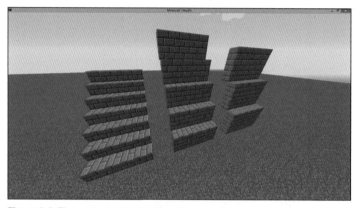

Figure 9-3: Three slanted walls with different slopes.

Constructing polygons with slanted walls

You can make all sorts of shapes by connecting slanted walls at different angles. Figure 9-4 shows four different polygons: a diamond, a parallelogram, a pentagon, and a hexagon.

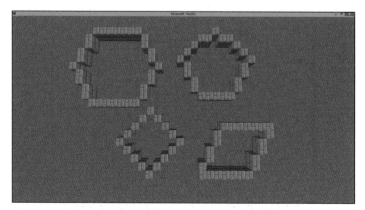

Figure 9-4: Interesting shapes that you can use for floor plans.

To build polygons like one of these, follow these steps:

1. **Visualize what the polygon will look like.**

   Figure 9-4 can help.

2. **Build one side.**

   The rest of the polygon will be built using this side as a guide. Count off the number of blocks if you need to — if the polygon includes another equal side, copy this side exactly.

3. **Complete the other sides of the polygon.**

   Pay particular attention to sides facing the same direction (parallel) and sides with the same length (congruent).

4. **Fix any mistakes.**

   If your polygon doesn't connect exactly right, recheck the length and angle of each side to figure out where the problem is so that you can fix it.

A few common polygons make for truly interesting buildings:

- ✔ **Triangle:** Triangles make good bases. A right triangle — essentially a rectangle cut in half — is particularly common because it's easy to build and integrate with other structures.

- ✔ **Rectangle:** Though rectangles are fairly generic building bases, they're still popular. You can make a rectangle base more interesting by rotating it a little (refer to the diamond in Figure 9-4).

- ✔ **Hexagon:** A hexagon has six sides — usually three sets of parallel sides (refer to Figure 9-4). Most are made with 2 normal lines and 4 slanted lines.

- ✔ **Octagon:** Eight-sided polygons are almost always created with 4 normal lines and 4 diagonal lines. These shapes are good for building large, expansive rooms. You can also build the diagonal sides shorter than the others, to make the octagon look more like a square with its corners chopped off.

Building Circles and Spheres

In a world where everything consists of squares and cubes, creating anything that's perfectly round is impossible. But if you have your heart set on circles or spheres, we have a trick: You can come close by stacking blocks.

This section shows you how to build circles and spheres so that you can make items such as round rooms and dome ceilings, for example.

Constructing a circle

Building a circle relies on techniques similar to those used when building with slanted lines — you make both with small segments of blocks. Figure 9-5 shows four different circles built using this method.

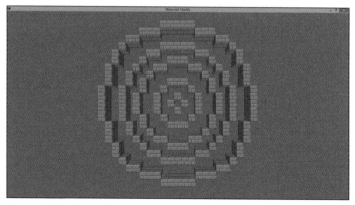

Figure 9-5: Circles made of blocks.

To build a circle like one of those shown in Figure 9-5, follow these steps:

1. **Construct the longest line segment.**

   It should be, at most, ⅓ the length of the circle's diameter.

2. **Construct a shorter line segment just behind the first one.**

3. **Continue making shorter lines, with the difference being smaller and smaller each time.**

   This step composes the arc at the top of the circle.

4. **Turn around and repeat.**

   When you estimate a circle in Minecraft, it should have 4-way symmetry: Whether you're looking north, south, east, or west, the circle should look the same. Thus, the process of constructing each side of the circle is exactly the same.

5. **Fix any lopsidedness.**

   If a segment looks too long, destroy a block at the end and extend the adjacent segment to fill the gap. If a segment looks too short, just do the same thing in reverse.

Even though you can't get a truly round circle, any rounded room tends to have the same effect.

Constructing a sphere

Spheres are much trickier to build than circles — it's a lot more difficult to estimate a three-dimensional rounded object than a flat one. However, there's a clever way you can build a sphere:

1. **Build a flat circle whose diameter is the same as your sphere's diameter.**

   This is the ring that will go around the middle of your sphere.

2. **Build two more circles in the same way, except that these circles are *vertical* (with their diameter perpendicular to the ground) and surround the sphere lengthwise and widthwise.**

   The result should be a cluster of three rings, each of which intersects the others twice.

3. **Fill out the sphere by building extra circles parallel to the first one, using the second and third circles as guides.**

Spheres can be used for all sorts of things — dome-shaped roofs, balloons, and blimps are just a few. Three-dimensional rounded objects are useful for making structures smoother and more elegant.

Implementing Fluids into Your Build

In addition to solid blocks, liquids such as water and lava make for eye-catching decorations. You can use water and lava buckets to make fountains, canals, moats, and more.

Understanding how fluids work

Water and lava have some interesting traits in the Minecraft world. They aren't just a single type of block — you can have both *source blocks* (the liquid in its still form) and *flowing blocks* (the liquid that flows away from the source blocks). Source blocks don't go away automatically, but flowing blocks disappear when the liquid's route changes.

To remove source block, place a block on top of it or pick it up with a bucket. However, be careful because flowing blocks can create source blocks if they flow into one another. (We talk more about creating source blocks in detail later on in the chapter.)

You can tell whether it's a source block because it's almost the size of a solid block and doesn't look like it's flowing in any direction, including down. You can gather source blocks with a bucket: Scoop up water or lava and take it somewhere else.

By placing water or lava blocks in your building, you can create a lot of neat structures. These liquids have a few interesting properties:

✔ **Source blocks spread north, south, east, west, and downward, but flow only into empty spaces.**

Water automatically flows to nearby spaces after a short delay.

✓ **Liquid blocks spread to the nearest dip in the land.**

If no solid block is directly under a flowing block, the liquid flows downward. If there's a hole in the ground somewhere up to 5 blocks away, the liquid flows toward it. If all else fails, the liquid flows north, south, east, and west.

✓ **When a block of liquid flows horizontally to a different space, the new liquid is slightly shorter.**

Water can travel as much as 8 blocks horizontally (including the source) before it becomes too thin to go any farther. Lava can only go for 4 — however, in the Nether dimension, lava travels much faster and farther. Also, if you try to place water in the Nether, it will immediately evaporate.

✓ **If a flowing block loses its connection to the liquid supporting it, it dries up.**

Lava takes much longer than water to do this, making it dangerous to work with.

✓ **If 2 water source blocks are 2 blocks apart, the blocks between them become source blocks.**

This method works only if the blocks between them have solid blocks underneath. Therefore, if you have a 2x2 well made of 4 source blocks, you can pick up part of the water with a bucket and the well will go right back to the way it was.

If you need a lot of water for your structure, build a well near the structure so that you have an infinite source of water nearby. This strategy doesn't work for lava, which isn't renewable — however, after you make it to the Nether, you can find huge oceans of lava that you can use.

These rules allow you to build a lot of interesting liquid structures in your world.

Building a fountain

Fountains are pretty popular in Minecraft. You can make one using either water or lava that falls from a few source blocks. Many times, a fountain is just a single block of water that spills down a few blocks and makes a neat pattern. However, you can use a few blocks of liquid in all sorts of creative ways. For example, Figure 9-6 shows a fountain with both water and lava streaming down the sides of a path.

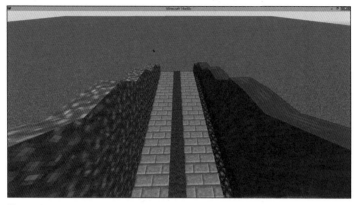

Figure 9-6: Liquid decorations.

To bend water and lava to your creation, follow these steps:

1. **Gather some buckets of water or lava.**

   You can use both water and lava, if you want — just make sure that the two never touch, or else they'll combine to form unwanted stone, cobblestone, or obsidian (depending on the arrangement).

2. **Place the liquid at the top of the stream you want to create.**

   Place more source blocks if there's a gap in the water.

3. **Block off any parts of the current that go somewhere you don't want them to.**

   For example, if a waterfall spills all over the ground, build a little cup around the base of the stream to contain it.

4. **Place blocks in the liquid's path to change its course.**

   Whether you use single blocks or trails, you can direct liquids around however you want. Try out several different arrangements in order to get the creation you want.

5. Repeat Steps 3 and 4 until you have the shape you like.

Add more source blocks, if you want.

Building structures underwater

If you've ever wanted to live under the sea, now's your chance. You just need to know a few things before you get started:

- ✓ You want your rooms to be free of water.
- ✓ You can hold your breath for only so long.
- ✓ You are slow when underwater.

It's tricky to build an underwater structure, but it can be done.

Obtaining the necessary gear

Your best bet for clearing out water is sponges, which can soak up a lot of water at a time and be dried out in a furnace. If you don't have many sponges, you'll want lots of cheap, easily destroyed blocks, like sand. Source blocks are destroyed by placing solid blocks inside them, so you can fill your rooms up with temporary blocks to blot out all the water.

However, you still have the problem of staying underwater and building effectively for an extended period. Fortunately, you can use an enchanting table to enchant armor with some useful abilities:

- ✓ **Respiration:** This enchantment is for your helmet that lets you hold your breath much longer and see clearly underwater. If you get the highest possible level (Respiration III), you can stay underwater for an extra 45 seconds without taking damage.

- ✓ **Aqua Affinity:** This enchantment, another one for your helmet, lets you destroy blocks underwater just as quickly as you can above water.

- ✓ **Depth Strider:** This enchantment is for your boots. With this enchantment, you can move much faster underwater.

The highest possible level (Depth Strider III) lets you move as fast as you can on land, though you can't sprint underwater.

Beginning the underwater construction

When you're ready, you can begin building your masterpiece under the sea. The process for underwater construction is a bit different if you've chanced upon some sponges. It turns out that getting sponges is very tricky, requiring that you go to a water temple. Sponges can be found in sponge rooms which are randomly generated in the water temple, or, one is dropped when you kill an elder guardian. If you have some sponges to use, just follow these steps:

1. **Go underwater and start building the exterior of your structure.**

   Construct all the floors, walls, and ceilings.

2. **Keep building until all the walls and ceilings are finished.**

   Make sure that no more water can enter your structure. If you miss a spot, don't worry — the problem will go away if you just patch up the part that's leaking.

3. **Enter your building.**

   It's probably full of water right now. Remember that water can't pass through doors, fence gates, and the like — you can build a gateway right out into the ocean, if you want.

4. **Place a furnace in your building.**

   You can ignore this step if you have a lot of dry sponges.

5. **Put sponges next to the water source blocks.**

   This step soaks up the water and converts your sponges into wet sponges.

6. **If water remains, put your wet sponges into the furnace.**

   By cooking wet sponges, you can dry them out so that they're ready to use again.

7. **Continue soaking up the water until it's all cleared out.**

8. **Destroy all the sponges.**

9. **Continue designing the interior of your structure.**

If you don't have sponges to follow these steps, you have to rely on a slower method:

1. **Grab the necessary building materials, along with a bunch of dirt or sand blocks.**

   Both dirt and sand have their advantages, but we recommend sand — it's affected by gravity, so it can easily complete Step 4. Besides, you can destroy whole columns of sand quickly by destroying the bottom block and immediately replacing it with a torch or pressure plate or another nonsolid block.

2. **Build the floors and walls of your structure.**

3. **Fill up the entire structure with the dirt or sand blocks.**

4. **Build the ceiling of your structure, and be sure to fill any gaps with dirt or sand.**

5. **Enter the structure.**

6. **Destroy all excess dirt and sand, revealing a water-free interior.**

7. **Get rid of any leftover water by picking it up with buckets, or by placing blocks in the sources.**

8. **Decorate the interior of your structure.**

No matter which of these two methods you pick, you can soon come up with a great-looking design in an interesting environment.

10

Implementing Gardens into Your World

In This Chapter

▶ Gathering and growing plants

▶ Constructing and furnishing gardens

▶ Adding gardens to a structure

*G*ardens add a natural flair to your Minecraft world, but creating them is quite a bit different from creating buildings. Plant life follows different rules than building blocks (such as cobblestone) follow. This chapter shows you how to find and gather the proper materials and build gardens of any sort.

Obtaining Plants

Minecraft has many different nature-themed blocks that you can collect and add to your garden — and unlike with stone or metal, you can find most of them aboveground. However, many plants can be found only in certain *biomes* — specific geographic areas such as plains or forests. So although you don't have to go underground, you do have to do a lot of exploring to find them.

You can use many different plants to build a garden, as described in this list:

   ✓ **Grass blocks:** Grass blocks are easy to find — they're all over the place in most biomes. When you give grass blocks enough light and maybe some bonemeal now and then to speed things along, they eventually spread to cover nearby dirt blocks. This is handy because you can lead a trail of grass to a lifeless patch of dirt so that you can start cultivating it.

Grass changes color depending on which biome it's in. If you don't want your garden to be greenish brown, stay away from hot biomes such as deserts and savannahs.

✔ **Tall grass:** You get regular grass by using bonemeal on grass blocks. If you then add more bonemeal to the grass, you end up with tall grass, which can then be collected using shears or a silk touch item.

✔ **Cacti:** Cacti, which you can find in deserts, are solid blocks and easy to harvest. Though cacti can be helpful additions to a garden, you should know a couple of facts about them: You can place cacti only on sand blocks, and you can't place them next to other blocks. And watch out because they hurt anything that touches them.

✔ **Mushrooms and mycelium:** Mushrooms sometimes look interesting in gardens, but they can really only survive in semi-darkness. Note that it doesn't have to be complete darkness, meaning that if it's a dim inside garden, it can look neat.

If you're just dying to have mushrooms in a brighter space, use bonemeal to turn your puny mushrooms into much more resilient giant mushrooms, making it so they can survive even in bright sunlight.

Mycelium isn't always a useful addition to gardens, because it can spread over grass and you can't grow much of anything on it. It turns out, however, that you can safely place mushrooms on mycelium, even in broad daylight.

✔ **Saplings and trees:** If a sapling has enough space, it grows into a tree. Minecraft has many different kinds of saplings (and therefore many different kinds of trees). You can choose different shapes and textures depending on what you want in your garden.

✔ **Crops:** Wheat, carrots, potatoes, pumpkins, and melons are useful additions to a garden. Even nether wart and cocoa bean pods can look good with decorative flowers, if you don't use too many of them.

✔ **Sugar cane:** This plant takes on the same color as the grass underneath it, and it can grow as much as 3 blocks high and you can manually place more sugarcane to make a larger stack. You can place sugar cane only next to water, so it's helpful for bordering pools and lakes.

✔ **Lily pads:** These plants, which are usually found in swamps, can be placed on top of water. They look pretty, but it turns out that you can actually walk over them, so you can use them to make a cool bridge. They can be found in Swamp biomes and can be broken with anything.

✔ **Vines:** You can hang vines on walls so that they hang down, like drapes. You can also climb them, which is helpful if you don't have a ladder. However, be sure to keep them under control, because they spread both downward and horizontally.

✔ **Flowers:** The most obvious item to add to a garden is flowers. You can find all kinds of flowers just about anywhere. (See Table 10-1.)

Table 10-1   Flowers and Their Habitats

Plant	Where to Find	Description
Allium	Flower Forest biomes	A round, purple flower
Azure Bluet	Plains and flower forests	A white bunch of flowers
Blue Orchid	Swamps	A thin, blue plant
Dandelion	Many biomes	A little yellow flower that appears commonly
Lilac	Forests	A group of small, purple flowers two blocks tall
Oxeye Daisy	Plains and flower forests	A classic white flower
Peony	Forests	A group of large, purple flowers two blocks tall
Poppy	Many biomes	A common little red flower

(continued)

Table 10-1 *(continued)*

Plant	Where to Find	Description
Rose Bush	Forests	A bush of red flowers two blocks tall
Sunflower	Special "sunflower plains"	A rare, large flower that always faces in the same direction
Tulip	Plains and flower forests	A small flower that may come in several different colors

If you want a plant that you can find only in a certain biome, you can go to that biome and use bonemeal on the grass. When a random cluster of plants appear, look for the ones you like, harvest those and take them back to your garden. (You may have to try this a few times before you get the flowers you wanted.)

Building Your First Garden

Creating a garden can be tricky — most plants can be placed only on top of solid blocks, so you end up with a flat, boring garden. If you'd rather have an interesting, elaborate garden, you need these three elements:

- ✔ **A well-planned layout**
- ✔ **A nice variety of plants**
- ✔ **A well-organized space**

Figure 10-1 shows an example of a garden — by following the advice in this section, you can invent and build your own.

Laying out your garden

The first thing to do is lay out your garden — you can't set up all your plants without having something to place them on. For some gardens, the layout is a simple patch of grass; other gardens may be a little more elaborate and use grass platforms connected with ladders or bridges.

Figure 10-1: A garden featuring many different crops.

To lay out your garden, follow these steps:

1. **Place patches of dirt where you want your greenery to be located.**

   Normally, you can't pick up grass blocks, so you have to place dirt blocks and then grow grass over them. However, if you have a lot of expendable resources, you can use the Silk Touch enchantment to obtain grass blocks directly.

2. **Construct borders, bridges, ladders, water, and anything else that isn't a plant of some kind.**

   Build these items early on so that you don't discover complications later.

3. **Use more dirt blocks to connect all patches of land with nearby grass.**

   As long as your grass has enough light, it spreads into your garden. Figure 10-2 shows grass spreading throughout a garden.

   Watching grass grow is exactly as boring as it sounds; work on other tasks while you wait for your garden to become green.

4. **Destroy all excess dirt or grass blocks.**

   When this step is done, you're ready to start planting.

Figure 10-2: Turning dirt blocks into grass blocks.

Arranging plants in a garden

After the basic plan for your garden is set up, you can start adding some plants to it. To do that, just follow these steps:

1. **Decide how much color you want in your garden.**

   Some people like gardens that are mostly green, with small bits of color here and there. Others like bright and vibrant colors everywhere. The color options are completely up to you. Just be sure to make your decision before you move to Step 2.

2. **Choose the plants you want to use.**

   Pick colors and shapes that go well together but don't overload your garden with too many different types of plants. See the section "Obtaining Plants," at the beginning of this chapter, for a list of some plants you can use.

3. **Decide where to place all your tall plants.**

   This decision includes cacti, trees, sugar canes, and tall flowers such as peonies. Keep in mind that you can't see shorter plants if they're obscured by too many tall ones. We like to place tall plants in small lines or curves to help define the shape of the garden.

4. **Decide which sections should have no plants.**

   You don't have to cover every single grass block with plants — always leave some room to walk around. You can even add a gravel road or two. After you know which spots you want to remain empty, you'll know where to place all the other plants you want to add.

5. **Place all your small, colorful plants.**

   Arrange these elements however you like — you can easily change them later.

6. **Fill the rest of the unused space with green plants.**

   Items such as ferns and tall grass work well for filling in gaps. Be sure not to fill in any areas you want to keep clear for paths or roads.

Integrating Gardens with Other Buildings

Gardens are usually combined with other structures, such as farmhouses or castles. You can even place a garden *inside* another structure. (Figure 10-3 shows a garden built in the middle of a mansion, for example.)

Figure 10-3: An interior garden.

The following sections show you how to create a garden that fits well with the rest of your world.

Constructing a border for a garden

If your buildings are walled off by design, your garden may be left out in the open, and without a border it may look unfinished.

It's up to you whether to add a border to your garden, but if you do, here are some tips regarding placement, choice of materials, and color preferences:

✓ **Use low borders:** Make the border short and simple — we recommend using noncubical blocks such as fences or slabs.

✓ **Build borders with fitting colors:** A garden doesn't exactly look natural when surrounded by iron blocks. Use natural-looking blocks such as leaves or wooden fences or soft, cold colors such as prismarine blocks.

✓ **Design the garden to match your chosen borders:** The border should blend with the garden for a natural look. For example, you might place tall plants along the inside of the border or leave a little space between the border and the plants.

Building a garden on another structure

Some gardens are planted on the ground, and others aren't. You can add a garden to a structure in many different ways. Here are just a few:

✓ **Build a garden on top of a building.**

Unless you live in a big city, you may not have seen a garden on top of a building, but they're pretty cool. You can build a garden on top of a roof — it looks good and gets plenty of light because it's still under the open sky.

✔ **Construct a garden on the inside corner of a building.**

Many buildings are more than simple rectangles — they can have multiple rooms and hallways with bends and turns. If the outside of your structure is looking bare, you can fill in the corners of those turns with a garden.

✔ **Add a garden that's half-indoors and half-outdoors.**

An indoor/outdoor garden isn't too hard to make. Just plant your garden and then place a floor around it. Only add walls and ceilings to part of the structure so that the garden is half indoors and half outdoors.

✔ **Create an indoor garden.**

This is Minecraft, so of course it's entirely possible to create an indoor garden. Use torches, glowstone, or lamps to light up the garden. If you want, surround it with wood or greenery.

✔ **Build simple flowerbeds or add just a few flowers or potted plants.**

A simple flowerbed is a pleasant detail to add to any structure, and you can make one with fewer than 10 blocks. Some flowers, a potted plant, or even a patch of grass can add the final touch to your building. Figure 10-4 shows an example of this idea.

Figure 10-4: Using plants to produce small decorations.

11

Exploring the Functions of Glass

In This Chapter

▶ Incorporating glass into your designs

▶ Mastering glassmaking basics

▶ Creating structural and decorative elements made of glass

▶ Working with glass of a different color

*G*lass almost always makes a structure look amazing and interesting. Of course, you can use glass to build windows, but you can also use it to build walls, floors, and roofs. You can get even more creative by making stained glass. Glass is an excellent way to decorate rooms and buildings. It's useful for windows or lights. You can also find different types and shapes of glass — glass panes, blocks, and stained glass, for example. In this chapter, you can find out how to make all of these things, and more. You also see how to use these things in your structure.

Planning How to Use Glass

Glass lets in natural light and makes rooms and buildings more attractive. When you make glass, you can make it in a few forms: blocks, panes, or stained glass. Before you start making glass, you should know how you want to use it and where you're going to put it. Yes, we're talking about planning . . . again. But it's important — if you don't plan, you won't know how many blocks or panes you need.

How do you want to use glass? The most obvious task to use glass for is to build a window. As in your real-life house, windows make a big difference in a room — they make everything lighter and brighter.

Let's say that you want to make a window in a room. The first thing you need to do is decide where you want to put it. Go outside and walk around your structure. Where do you think a window would look best? Or look around inside — are there rooms that look a little dark and could use more light? Or maybe you have a room that would just look nice with a window as decoration.

When you find a place for a window, look at the other side of the wall. For example, if you found a good place for a window on the outside of your building, go inside and look at the same part of the wall to make sure that the glass works there as well.

You don't want the outside of your structure to look crowded, so don't feel like you have to have glass. If it's not a fit for this building, you can plan to have it in your next one.

Making Glass

Glass blocks are cool because they offer so many creative, decorative, and useful options. As we mention earlier in this chapter, you can make a few types of glass. We cover glass blocks and panes in this section. (Stained glass is described toward the end of this chapter.)

How and when you use glass blocks or panes is up to you, but generally blocks are better for large projects (such as building a wall or barrier) and panes are better for smaller projects (such as windows). But it's perfectly fine to use them any way you like.

Follow these steps to make 1 block of glass:

1. **Break a block of sand, and pick it up by walking over it.**

   You can use regular or red sand — the kind of sand you choose doesn't have an effect on the glass itself.

2. **Mine coal and pick it up.**

   For help with mining, see Chapter 4.

3. **Go back to your house, and then right-click on the furnace to access it.**

   You use the furnace to smelt sand into glass. For information on furnaces, check out Chapter 4.

4. **Place the sand in the top box and the coal in the bottom box.**

5. **Wait until the sand is smelted, and then take the glass that appears.**

Glass panes are similar to glass blocks, but they look more realistic — like the windows you're used to seeing in your real-life house. Panes are also different from blocks because you can break them and pick them up as an item, just in case you mess up. (When you break glass blocks, they don't drop as an item; they just disappear.)

Making Windows

If you're using glass for windows, make sure to place the windows where they will get light. For example, if you place the window too low, it will be difficult for the window to let light in. We don't mean to say that it won't get *any* light, but it won't get as much light as if you were to place it higher.

Large-scale windows look good but take some time to build. In the end, it's worth every second. As we've said throughout this book, planning is a big part of building anything, and these big windows definitely require some planning. You can start by asking yourself these questions:

✔ **How large do you want the window to be? Will it be an entire wall?** Or will it be narrow and tall or wide and short? This question is extremely important because it not only helps you plan out your building, but also helps you calculate the amount of materials you need to complete the build.

↙ **Do you want the window to resemble something, such as a tree or a specific shape?** If you want the window to look like something else, check out the later section "Using Stained Glass." Stained glass is the easiest way to create a specific design with glass.

↙ **Do you want the window to face a specific direction?** For example, do you want to be able to see the sun rise, or would you prefer to see the sun set? Is there a particular feature you want to see (such as a farm or a garden)? If so, put that in the plan.

You make a large window the same way you make a small window (see the earlier section "Making Glass" for instructions). The only difference is how many blocks you break to make room for the glass. If you're building a big window as you build your structure, you'll just need more glass blocks or panes than you would for smaller windows.

When you want to add a window to your building, you need to make the glass (see the earlier section "Making Glass"), build a place for the window (knock out part of the wall), and then place the glass in the wall. A good height to place a window is at eye level — 2 blocks high, in other words.

Here's how to do those things:

1. **Smelt as many glass blocks or panes as you need for your window.**

2. **Take the glass to where you want to have the window and keep them in the inventory.**

3. **Break as many wall blocks as you need for your window.**

   Figure 11-1 shows how to do this.

   To break a block, click on it and hold until it breaks.

4. **Place (right click) the glass in the holes in the wall.**

We suggest making windows at least 2 blocks wide so that you have enough light.

Figure 11-1: Creating a space for your window.

How does your new window look? Not bad for your first one, right? With one window under your belt, you can now make and add as many as you want. Try making an even bigger window the next time or maybe a stained glass window. (We talk about stained glass later in this chapter.)

Using Glass as Decorative Trim

Any building that uses one only type of block (such as cobblestone, brick, or wood) may look boring because nothing stands out. You can add trim to your building to make it more interesting.

You apply trim when you use one main type of block to build something like a wall (say, cobblestone) and then you use another type of block (say brick) to outline it. The thing is, glass is a perfectly respectable choice for decorative trim, as Figure 11-2 plainly shows.

Figure 11-2: A cobblestone/glass combination.

Before you add trim to your building, you first have to have a building. For instructions on how to make a building, check out Chapter 4.

When you're choosing what kind of block to use as trim, think about which types go together. (More on that in Chapter 7.) For example, cobblestone is gray and doesn't really stand out much. Glass is clear (unless you're using stained glass, which we get to in a minute), and it doesn't really stand out by itself, either. But if you put cobblestone and glass together in the same wall, it looks pretty good. The rough cobblestone next to the smooth glass provides a nice contrast.

To use glass (or any type of block, really) as trim, you have a lot of options: You can place it at the base of your house (the bottom row of blocks), add it to the corners or top row of your building, or put it around a door to make a frame. You can even make a stripe in the middle of your structure. It would look pretty awesome to have a whole row of glass blocks in the middle of your building (and you'd have plenty of light, too!).

To give your building a 3D effect, put trim blocks 1 block in front of the main blocks.

Using Glass as Flooring

You're going to love this idea. Because glass is transparent, you can place lava or water underneath your house, place glass blocks over it, and walk safely through your house. We tell you how to make both.

Bringing the heat

Lava looks neat as a floor, but of course you can't walk on lava or else you'd catch on fire. If you put glass blocks over the lava, though, you create an appealing effect. You need enough glass blocks to make three items for a lava/glass floor: your floor, a bucket, and lava.

If you're not sure how much glass you need, count your floor's area in blocks, and that's how many glass blocks you need.

Make that number of glass blocks (see the instructions earlier in this chapter) and you're set to go.

In this situation, you use glass blocks because they look much better than glass panes. Glass blocks are also a better idea because if you were to use glass panes, then you would fall through your floor!

The number of buckets you need depends on how big your floor is and how far your lava source is. If you have big floors or faraway lava, make and take several buckets; if you have small floors or a nearby lava source, you can probably get away with using just one.

There are two ways to find lava:

✔ **Start a mine.** Be careful! When you mine, it puts you at a high risk of falling into lava, which would probably kill you. (See Chapter 4 to get the scoop on mining and the dangers of lava.)

✔ **Find it aboveground.** Doing so is rare, and it will require some exploring to find it. If you decide to accept the challenge, start by looking by beaches.

Now you have your buckets, glass blocks, and lava. It's time to start building! Follow these steps to create the lava/glass floor:

1. **Dig a hole 2 blocks deep as wide and as long as your floor.**

   This will be the lava pit.

2. **Place one row of glass on the top of the ground floor so that you can walk across the lava pit.**

   Depending on how large the floor is, you may need multiple rows. Building these rows allows you to fill your pit with lava safely, without burning yourself. To see an example, look at Figure 11-3.

3. **Climb out of your hole by making a staircase.**

   To get out of this pit, build block stairs as shown in Figure 11-4.

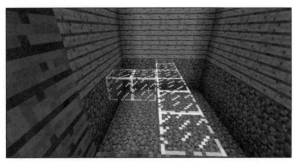

Figure 11-3: How to not burn yourself when making the floor.

Figure 11-4: Climbing out of your hole.

4. **Stand on your glass rows and fill your pit with lava, starting from the corner and moving to the opposite corner.**

   Make the lava only 1 block high so that you can still place glass above it for the floor.

   One bucket of lava fills 1 block of your lava pit. When you pour lava into a block, it spreads out a little bit and gets in some of the other blocks. That's okay. Just keep using a whole bucket in each block and it will work itself out.

5. **When the lava pit is full, place glass blocks over it.**

   Make sure that you don't leave any holes in the floor, because if you were to fall, it might kill you!

We really love the look of a lava floor. What do you think? Figure 11-5 shows what one looks like when it's done.

Figure 11-5: A lava-and-glass floor adds a little spice to your floor.

Going with the flow

Water flooring is pretty much the same as lava flooring, except that it uses water instead of lava. The water makes a pretty cool effect. To make a glass floor with water under it, you need glass blocks, a bucket, sand, and water.

You can use the advice in the "Bringing the heat" section to figure out how many glass blocks to make. And, like the lava floor, the number of buckets you need depends on how big the floor is and how far away the water source is.

Finding sand and water is quite a bit easier than finding lava (aboveground, anyway) — just go to a beach (and don't forget your buckets).

When you get to the beach, right-click to use the bucket to scoop up water. To gather sand, left-click to break the sand and walk over it to pick it up. Make sure to pick up enough sand to cover the floor. Take the sand and water back to your building and you're ready to get started.

Here's how to create the water/glass floor:

1. **Make a hole as long and as wide as the floor by digging 2 blocks down.**

2. **Jump down into the hole.**

3. **Place the water into the hole, filling the hole 1 block high.**

   It's okay to let the water touch you, because, unlike lava, water won't kill you.

4. **Place one block of any kind in front of you so that you can jump up to the surface, as shown in Figure 11-6.**

   After you're out of your hole, you can destroy the block that you used.

5. **Place glass blocks over the water (1 block high is enough).**

Figure 11-6: Leave a way to get out of the hole.

Check for holes in the floor, or else you might end up swimming! Figure 11-7 shows a finished water floor.

Figure 11-7: A water-and-glass floor makes it easy to walk on water.

Building Glass Ceilings

Do you like looking at the moon, clouds, or a nice blue sky? Need a little more natural light than your windows offer? If you have a 1-story house, a glass ceiling looks nice and gives you a pretty good view. You can see an example in Figure 11-8. Of course, if you have a 2-story house and you put a glass ceiling above the first floor, you're looking up, into the rooms above.

Figure 11-8: A glass ceiling.

If a glass ceiling is right for you, follow these steps to build one:

1. **Break the ceiling of your building (if you already have one made).**

   If you don't have a ceiling yet, you can skip to Step 2.

2. **Make enough glass to cover the room.**

3. **Place the glass above you, making a ceiling.**

   Chapter 4 explains how to make ceilings.

There you go! Now you have a glass roof that gives you plenty of natural light and looks good, too.

Using Stained Glass

Stained glass is a helpful way to decorate your house or building. It's artsy, colorful, and creative (see Figure 11-9). To make stained glass, you need dye and glass blocks. You have to make dye yourself.

Figure 11-9: A stained glass picture.

Table 11-1 describes how to make the color you're looking for.

Table 11-1	Dye Colors	
Dye Color	**What to Use**	**How to Make It**
Red	Poppy, red tulip, or rose bush	Place the poppy, red tulip, or rose bush in any box on the crafting table.
Orange	Orange tulip	Place the orange tulip in crafting table, using any box.
Yellow	Dandelion sunflower	Place the dandelion sunflower in any box of the crafting table.
Green	Cactus	Smelt the cactus in a furnace, giving you green dye.
Blue	Lapis lazuli ore	Mine the lapis lazuli ore and smelt it in a furnace.
Light blue	Blue orchid	Place the blue orchid in any box of the crafting table.
Magenta	Lilac allium	Place the lilac allium in any box of the crafting table.
Pink	Peony or pink tulips	Place the peony or pink tulip into any box in the crafting table.

Dye Color	What to Use	How to Make It
White	Bonemeal	Place the bone meal in any box of the crafting table.
Light gray	Azure bluet, oxeye daisy, white tulip	Place the azure bluet, oxeye daisy, or white tulip into any box of the crafting table.
Black	Ink sac from squid	Squids drop 0 to 3 ink sacs when killed.
Brown	Cocoa plants	Found in dungeons, or growing on jungle trees.
Cyan dye	Green dye + blue dye	Place green and blue dyes in any box of crafting table.
Purple dye	Red dye + blue dye	Place red and blue dyes in any box of the crafting table.
Gray dye	Black dye + white dye	Place black and white dye in any box of the crafting table.
Lime dye	Green dye + white dye	Place green and white dye in any box of the crafting table.

Ready to make some art? Follow these instructions to make stained glass:

1. **Make 8 glass blocks.**

2. **Make 1 dye of any color.**

    See Table 11-1.

3. **Place the 8 glass blocks into the crafting table, filling all boxes except the center one.**

4. **Place your dye in the center box.**

5. **Take the 8 stained glass blocks that the crafting table gives you.**

You can build with stained glass the same way you'd build with regular glass, but it has the added value of adding color to your buildings. Let your imagination go wild and use multiple stained glass blocks to make a picture in a floor, wall, or ceiling.

To make stained glass panes, you'll need six glass blocks that are the same color. Place those six glass blocks into your crafting table, filing the bottom and middle rows. Take the 16 glass panes in exchange for the stained glass blocks, and you're finished!

12

Implementing Redstone into Your Building

*R*edstone refers to an interesting group of items and blocks based around the versatile redstone dust item. Redstone-based blocks act as wiring and triggers — they let you create programs that run machines, move blocks around, and basically do some truly amazing things. You can use redstone to improve your buildings and make them more dynamic (and more fun) — this chapter shows you some ways to do that.

Understanding the Essential Concepts of Redstone

Redstone is cool because you can use it to add moving parts and automatic devices (such as pistons and elevators) to your buildings. These types of features make structures look a lot more interesting. You find redstone deep in caves and when you break it, it drops 4 to 5 redstone dust.

Before you jump in and start using redstone, you need to know two things: how the different redstone-based blocks work and what they can do for you.

After you get the hang of working with redstone, you can do some pretty complicated things with it. First, though, you should tackle the basics. This list describes the important elements of redstone:

✔ **Redstone dust:** This is Minecraft's version of wiring. It transfers redstone power (an electricity-like force created by machines such as levers and buttons) from one place to another. You can place redstone dust on any solid block, and it automatically connects with adjacent redstone dust. You can then create trails of dust to transfer power around your world. Redstone dust can even climb up and down, running up ridges that are 1 block tall, as shown in Figure 12-1.

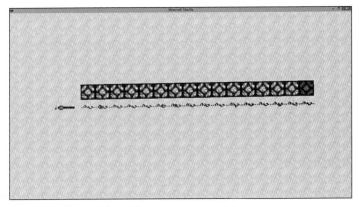

Figure 12-1: Transmitting redstone power upwards

If you place redstone dust so that it runs directly into a solid block, that block can become powered and activate every device adjacent to it. Powered redstone dust also powers the block below it. You should know, though, that blocks powered in this way cannot power more redstone dust in turn.

Redstone dust can carry power only for a distance of 15 blocks before its current dies out. When you get the hang of working with redstone, you can discover some ways to use this to your advantage. (Recall that you can obtain redstone in mines and it drops 4-5 redstone dust when you break it.)

✔ **Redstone torches:** The torch is an extremely useful device, and it's the starting point for many different machines. You can place redstone torches either on the top or side of a block. Redstone torches constantly power all adjacent mechanisms unless they're turned off and redstone torches turn off if the block that they're placed on is powered. This makes redstone torches useful for making circuits so that you can turn things on and off. For example, you can make a piston retract instead of extend when you push a button. Also, if a solid block is directly above an active redstone torch, the torch powers that block, charging everything adjacent to it. Figure 12-2 shows an example of how you might use a redstone torch.

Figure 12-2: Various functions of redstone torches.

✔ **Redstone repeaters:** The repeater is a common feature in the world of electronics, where you often need a device that can receive a signal and then retransmit it a higher level, sending the signal on its merry way with a bit more oomph behind it. In Minecraft, you create a repeater using three stone, two levers, and one redstone dust. The back end of the repeater receives power, which is then transferred to the front of the repeater after a short delay. A repeater can power either machines or blocks, and you can apply the Use Item button to change the length of the delay. These are interesting devices you can place, facing any of four directions.

The redstone repeater's primary use is to delay redstone pulses. However, you can also use it as a one-way street for redstone power, and a repeater's ability to power blocks makes it invaluable for charging multiple machines at one time. Though redstone dust can travel only 15 blocks, you can use redstone repeaters to break up a trail of dust to easily make it send current over long distances.

✔ **Pistons:** These blocks can push other blocks. When powered, the piston extends a wooden arm 1 block in some direction, pushing up to 12 blocks along with it. To craft a piston you need three wood planks, four cobblestone, an iron ingot, and one redstone dust.

If a piston tries to push a slime block, it also pushes every block adjacent to the slime block. However, the twelve block rule still applies, meaning you can't push a slime block if there are twelve or more blocks stuck to it. To avoid worrying about this, you can surround the slime block with the following blocks that don't stick to slime blocks: furnaces, note blocks, and obsidian.

✔ **Sticky pistons:** These are variants on the traditional piston model and can be made by crafting a piston with a slime ball. Sticky pistons can push blocks just like normal pistons, but when the piston's arm retracts, it pulls back the block in front of it. Like pistons, sticky pistons can pull many blocks at a time if all the blocks are connected by slime blocks.

✔ **Levers:** A lever is a simple way to make redstone power and can be crafted with a stick and one cobblestone. When selected with the Use Item button, your lever switches on and starts to transmit redstone power as well as powering every mechanism adjacent to it as well as the block it's placed on. If you engage the lever again, you can shut off the power.

✔ **Buttons:** Of all of the redstone devices out there, buttons are by far the easiest to craft; all you need is either one wood or one stone. When you use buttons, they transmit power for a short time and then shut off again. Again, you can make buttons either out of stone or wood — both materials function the same, except that you can also activate a wooden button by shooting it with an arrow.

✔ **Tripwires:** These work by laying string in a straight line between two tripwire hooks. When the string is stepped on or destroyed, the tripwire hooks activate just as buttons do. (You can make tripwire hooks using one iron, one stick, and one plank in a vertical line; to defuse a tripwire, use shears.)

✔ **Pressure plates** provide power to themselves and the block below when something lands on them. This makes them useful for powering automatic machines. For example, you can set them up so that you can make things happen just by walking along a line of pressure plates.

You can make pressure plates out of wood, stone, gold, iron, or all of the above. If you make a wooden pressure plate, you can activate it with anything, including arrows, thrown items, mobs, and players. If you make a stone pressure plate, you can activate it only with large entities such as mobs and players.

Golden and iron pressure plates give off a redstone charge whose intensity depends on how many entities are on them — the more entities on the pressure plate, the farther the resulting current can travel along a wire of redstone dust. Gold pressure plates gain charge quickly as more entities are added, whereas iron pressure plates require a lot more weight.

Figure 12-3 shows a typical layout for a few redstone devices.

Figure 12-3: Redstone devices and their connections.

Applying Redstone to Your Build

Players use redstone for many things, from automatic machines to advanced computers. But how can you use redstone to improve your building projects? This section helps you find out.

Using redstone in lighting

Redstone lamps can be turned on and off, as opposed to normal torches and lights that can only be covered up or destroyed. Redstone lamps are helpful when you're building things such as theaters, bathrooms, and any other structures where you think a light switch would be handy.

To design a redstone-powered light, follow these steps:

1. **Place redstone lamps wherever you want the lights to be.**

   Redstone lamps are the simplest form of redstone-based light and provide light only when powered. They are crafted by surrounding a glowstone block. You can also use a piston to cover up a redstone lamp when it's on to create a sort of shudder effect when you deactivate the piston.

2. **Add a lever to the wall.**

   Place the lever somewhere so that the space just behind the wall is empty.

3. **Behind the wall, place a trail of redstone dust that leads to all the lamps.**

   If there's redstone dust trail right behind the block holding the lever, you can flip the lever to turn the lamps on or off.

Assembling redstone doors

Though the normal wooden and iron doors are useful, you can use pistons to build all sorts of neat redstone-powered doors. There are a lot of different door designs. A good basic one is 2 blocks tall and 1 block wide, as shown in Figure 12-4.

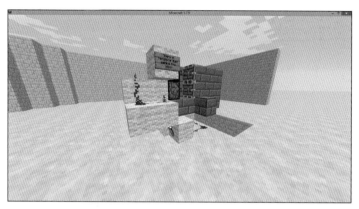

Figure 12-4: A simple redstone door.

Essentially, the pressure plates power the redstone below, which powers the block the redstone torch is on, thus deactivating it and both sticky pistons. So when the pressure plate is stepped on, both sticky pistons retract and open the wall.

If you want to build a 2-x-2 door, the process isn't much different — just add two more pistons and power them in exactly the same way, creating 4 blocks that pull apart and push together, like a sliding door. As for the placement of your new pistons, you have two options — you can place one piston at the top and bottom or one on either side.

Lastly, Figure 12-5 shows part of the redstone apparatus that surrounds a 3-x-3 door. The door is made up of 8 blocks in a ring. When you open the door, all the blocks are pulled apart in different directions. The challenge here is getting the redstone to connect to every single one of the pistons — it requires some fancy redstone tricks, but it's doable with some practice.

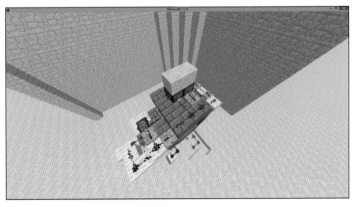

Figure 12-5: A 3-x-3 redstone door.

Designing redstone-powered farms

An automatic farm is always a good addition to your home. It's a much easier way to farm different plants, and you can even farm monsters to obtain loot easily.

Many players like to use redstone to automatically harvest plants and crops. For example, a melon farm works by planting stalks, waiting for them to grow, and seeing them create melon blocks in random adjacent spaces. You can speed up the harvesting of the created melon blocks with redstone power — just follow these steps:

1. **Plant a row of melon stalks.**

2. **Surround the stalks with blocks so that each stalk has only a single space to grow melon blocks on.**

3. **Place downward-facing sticky pistons 2 blocks above where the melon blocks will be.**

4. **Attach the sticky pistons to a single button.**

   When you push the button, the sticky pistons pull the melon blocks up and break them into items.

Redstone can be a great help at harvest time, but it can also help during the regular growing season. Take wheat, for example. Wheat tends to be difficult to grow; it's one of those crops that can benefit from the judicious use of bonemeal. Now picture a device that would apply the necessary bonemeal and then harvest the bumper crop of wheat you produce. Such a device would look much like the one shown in Figure 12-6.

Figure 12-6: The wiring of a wheat farm.

Basically, all three dispensers shown in Figure 12-6 contain bonemeal and grow the stalks to their full height. (So why are there *three* dispensers? It turns out it takes three bonemeal to guarantee that wheat fully grows.) After the dispensers activate and grow the wheat, the piston activates and destroys the wheat, turning it into items you can collect.

To use the machine, all you need to do is hold the Use Item button while holding seeds in the inventory and looking at the top of the dirt block. By rapidly planting and growing seeds and then collecting their items, you can get tons of wheat fast.

To build a machine like this bonemeal dispenser, follow these steps:

1. **Place an upward-facing piston on the ground.**

2. **Power the piston with a redstone torch.**

3. **Place a dirt block on the piston's extended arm.**

4. **Put some water near the dirt block.**

5. **Till the dirt block with a garden hoe.**

6. **Surround the top of the dirt block with dispensers, and fill the dispensers with bonemeal.**

7. **Add a pressure plate next to the dirt block.**

   You're going to stand on the pressure plate to activate it.

8. **Create a redstone loop — a redstone contraption that constantly goes back and forth between two positions. (Refer to the far left side of Figure 12-6.)**

9. **Hook up the loop so that it connects to both the dispensers and the redstone torch, but only when the pressure plate is pushed down.**

   This step can be tricky if you don't have a lot of experience with redstone. The design shown in Figure 12-6, does it by hooking up the pressure plate to a second piston, which pushes a block that completes the circuit.

Being inventive with redstone

The redstone devices we show you in this chapter aren't the only ones you can create. Try out ideas for any sort of dynamic machine you want — if you're in Survival mode, use a separate Creative mode world to test your ideas, if you want. Why not try building a bridge that pops out of the water when a pressure plate is triggered? Or a treasure chest system that sorts itself? Redstone can be a lot of fun, and it's worth using whenever you want your structures to be more interesting. To read even more about the ins and outs of redstone, check out *Minecraft Redstone For Dummies,* Portable Edition.

Concealing Redstone in Your Building

Adding redstone to your structure is fun, but it can create complications. What if your circuit doesn't fit in the structure? What if you don't want to see its inner workings — just its output?

Redstone contraptions often take up a lot of space. And they rarely coincide with the style of your building, so you may want them to work from a hidden location. To do that, just follow these tips:

✓ **Use powered blocks:** Remember that you can power a block by hitting it with redstone the right way. You can even transmit redstone current through walls, as well as floors and ceilings, although those are a bit trickier. If you want to activate something inside a room, you can keep all the circuitry outside the room and still make it work.

✓ **If you have no space for redstone, take it underground:** An underground circuit is useful for connecting things without showing all the technical stuff. (Remember, you can transmit redstone current through floors.)

✓ **Build vertically:** This is a tricky concept. Usually, when players first start using redstone, they build all their circuits flat against the ground — why not? It's easy. But if you really want your redstone to fit in any space, it helps to build *vertically*, transferring power upward instead of sideways. Powered blocks are extremely useful here, too. For example, you can use lots of redstone torches and redstone repeaters to carry a charge up through various powered blocks. It isn't a super-easy concept to grasp, but the more you practice building redstone flat against a wall, the easier it is — and you'll discover its many uses.

13

Using Lighting

. . . .

In This Chapter

▶ Finding the right type of lighting to use

▶ Building light sources into the structure

. . . .

*A*fter you've completely built a structure, you may notice that it's a bit dark inside and outside. Don't fret: This chapter tells you exactly how to add some light to a building.

Determining a Light Source

If you're in the dark about what might work best as a light source, don't worry. This section shines a little light on that topic. You have plenty of options to choose from, such as torches, glowstone, and lava, to name only a few.

Block light sources

As you can see throughout this book, Minecraft uses lots of different kinds of blocks. Some of them — glowstone, redstone lamp, and netherrack, to be specific — give off light. The next few sections dive into the specifics of each block light type.

Glowstone

Glowstone is a common way to produce light. To make glowstone, you need 4 glowstone dust — which makes sense. As for how to get hold of glowstone dust, that's a bit more complicated.

You can get glowstone dust one of three ways: Trade a villager for it, kill a witch, or mine it from the Nether. Note that not all villagers trade glowstone, but some do. If you're having trouble finding a villager willing to trade glowstone dust, move on to Option # 2: killing a witch.

A witch is easy to spot — the purple robe and the black pointy hat are dead giveaways. A witch is a hostile mob, and its attacks are long-distance, using splash potions as weapons. The best way to kill a witch is stay out of range of splash potions and use a bow and arrow.

When you succeed in killing a witch, she drops 1 to 3 different types of items. The booty may include a glass bottle, glowstone dust, gunpowder, redstone, a spider eye, a stick, or sugar. As to the size of the booty, you can get as little as 1 and as many as 6 of each item.

To mine glowstone, you'll need to venture into the Nether. (The Nether is explained in detail in the "Netherrack" section, later in this chapter.) After you arrive in the Nether, walk around and explore until you find glowstone. Then, all you have to do is mine it (left click). It will drop 2 to 4 glowstone dust.

After you have 4 glowstone dust, it's time to make glowstone. Here's how to do it:

1. **Open the crafting table.**

2. **Place the glowstone dust into the crafting table, with one in the left bottom box, one in the left middle box, one in the center box, and one in the bottom middle box, as shown in Figure 13-1.**

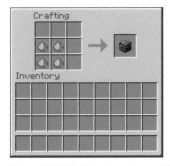

Figure 13-1: Making glowstone with glowstone dust.

3. **Take the glowstone block in exchange for the glowstone dust.**

Glowstone is a useful block for lighting a room. You can build with it or simply place it in a corner that needs a bit of extra light. You can also place glowstone blocks outside to light the exterior of buildings or perhaps a pathway.

Redstone lamps

Redstone lamps are powered by redstone torches — no surprise there — and thus are made using a process quite different from the one you'd use to make a glowstone block. To make a redstone lamp, you need 1 glowstone block and 4 redstone dust. You're probably an old hand at making glowstone blocks (if you've read the preceding section). As for the redstone dust, you get that by mining redstone and then smelting it in a furnace.

When you've gathered the glowstone block and 4 redstone dust, follow these instructions to make a redstone lamp:

1. **Open the crafting table and place the glowstone in the center box.**

2. **Place the redstone dust in the crafting table, with 1 redstone dust in the left middle box, 1 in the top middle box, 1 in the bottom middle box, and 1 in the right middle box, as shown in Figure 13-2.**

3. **Take the redstone lamp in exchange for the glowstone and the redstone dust.**

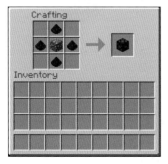

Figure 13-2: Making a redstone lamp.

You may have noticed that the redstone lamp isn't very bright. That's because you haven't powered it yet. To power a redstone lamp, you need a redstone torch. And to make a redstone torch, you need a stick and 1 redstone dust.

You can make a stick by placing 2 wooden planks into the crafting table, with 1 in the middle bottom box and the other in the center box.

With the stick and redstone dust in hand, follow these instructions to make a redstone torch:

1. **Place the redstone dust in the center box of the crafting table.**

2. **Place the stick in the bottom middle box, as shown in Figure 13-3.**

3. **Take the torch in exchange for the stick and redstone dust.**

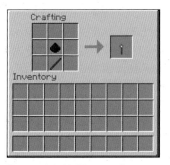

Figure 13-3: Making a redstone torch. _____

Right-click to place the torch next to the redstone lamp, and — voilà! — the lamp lights up. You have a working redstone lamp, just like the one shown in Figure 13-4. Nice, huh?

Netherrack

Netherrack doesn't glow like glowstone or lamps. Instead, you have to set netherrack on fire to get its light. To get netherrack, you have to go on a bit of an adventure — through a nether portal.

Figure 13-4: Redstone lamp.

To create a nether portal, you need 16 obsidian. You can get it in one of two ways: Mine it or make it. Chapters 4 and 7 explain both.

When you have 16 obsidian, you can make a portal by following these instructions:

1. **Place 4 obsidian blocks on the ground wherever you want to locate the base of the portal.**

2. **Stack 4 more blocks vertically on each side of the portal.**

3. **Place the last 4 obsidian blocks at the top, connecting the two sides.**

   Figure 13-5 shows a completed nether portal.

Figure 13-5: Nether portal.

The nether portal doesn't let you through if you don't activate it first by using steel and flint. To make steel and flint, you need 1 iron ingot and 1 flint. You can make an iron ingot by smelting an iron ore, but obtaining flint is a little more difficult. To get flint, you need to mine gravel. Mining gravel has a 10 percent chance of dropping flint instead of a gravel block, so it might take a while.

After you have the iron ingot and flint in hand, the rest is a piece of cake:

1. **Open the crafting table and place the iron ingot in the left middle box.**

2. **Place the flint in the center box of the crafting table, as shown in Figure 13-6.**

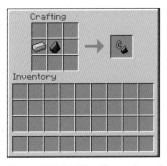

Figure 13-6: Making flint and steel.

3. **Take the steel and flint in exchange for the iron ingot and the flint.**

To activate the nether portal, have your steel and flint ready and right-click on an obsidian block that's a part of the portal. A purple misty wall appears inside the portal, as shown in Figure 13-7. Now, your portal is activated!

Before you go into the Nether, make sure that you have a pickaxe with you so that you can mine the netherrack.

Ready? Jump into the nether portal so that you can teleport to the Nether. When you arrive, step out of the portal, but watch out for fire and lava.

Figure 13-7: A completed nether portal.

When you exit the portal, look down at your feet. See the red/pink blocks you're standing on? That's netherrack. Take out your pickaxe and mine as much as you think you need for the lighting.

When you've gathered as much netherrack as you need, jump back into the portal to teleport back to where you came from. Take the netherrack to the spot where you want light and set it on fire using the flint and steel you made earlier. (Just right-click to spark the fire.) Figure 13-8 shows a lit netherrack.

Figure 13-8: Using netherrack as lighting.

When you place netherrack and light it, stand back and watch it for a minute or two, to ensure that the fire doesn't spread elsewhere from the netherrack. You don't want to come home one day and have your structure burned down!

Placing Lava

Lava is an interesting way to light a building, but don't use it if your structure is made from flammable blocks. For example, if the structure is made of wooden planks, reconsider using lava as a light source, unless you want a *big* bonfire. But, if your house is made out of stone, lava works just fine.

For a lava light, you need lava. Lava is placed randomly above and below ground, so you can't go to a specific spot and immediately find it. You'll just have to explore to find lava.

After you find lava, follow these steps:

1. **Fill the bucket with lava by holding the bucket and right-clicking.**

2. **Create an area for holding the lava in place, as shown in Figure 13-9.**

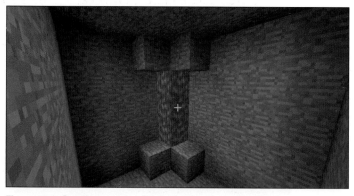

Figure 13-9: Creating a space for the lava.

Do this so that the lava doesn't spread everywhere and cause a problem.

3. **Right-click to place the lava where you want it.**

4. **Step back and make sure that lava isn't spreading everywhere.**

If it is, don't worry — simply place a block where you placed the lava and it will go away. You will have to replace the lava, but that's better than lava destroying your structure.

You can also add glass around the lava to make it safer. For more information on lava, look to Chapter 11.

Using Nonblock Lighting

Any lighting option that doesn't come from a block is a *nonblock light*. For example, a torch is nonblock lighting because it's not a block. In fact, many players use torches for light.

To make a torch, you need 1 stick and 1 coal (or charcoal). When you've gathered both, you can make a torch by following these instructions:

1. **Open the crafting table and place the stick in the lowest middle box.**

2. **Place the coal or charcoal in the center box, as shown in Figure 13-10.**

3. **Take the four torches in exchange for the stick and coal or charcoal.**

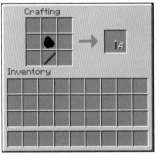

Figure 13-10: Making a torch.

You can place a torch either on a wall or on the floor. When placing a torch, don't worry about catching anything else on fire — torches are perfectly safe.

The other type of nonblock lighting is fire. To create fire, use flint and steel (see the earlier section "Netherrack") on a flammable block.

Here are the flammable blocks in Minecraft:

- Bookshelves
- Coal blocks
- Fences
- Hay bales
- Leaves
- Tall grass
- TNT
- Vines
- Wood
- Wooden blocks
- Wooden planks
- Wool

Making a Lamppost

Another option for lighting your way is by lamppost. You can make a lamppost using glowstone and 4 wooden fences.

The fence-making part is pretty easy:

1. **Gather four wooden planks.**

2. **Place one wooden plank in the crafting table's center box, and another in the bottom row's middle box.**

3. **Repeat step two for the remaining two planks.**

4. **Place six sticks in your crafting table, filling the middle and bottom rows.**

5. **Take the two wooden fences in exchange for the sticks.**

Now that you know how to make a wooden fence, you can start making a lamppost! Follow these steps to make a lamppost:

1. **Stack three wooden fences on top of each other, as shown in Figure 13-11.**

Figure 13-11: Start by stacking 3 wooden fences on top of each other.

2. **Place the last wooden fence on the side of the top fence, as shown in Figure 13-12.**

Figure 13-12: Use the last fencepost to make the hanger for the lamp.

3. **Place a glowstone block or redstone lamp below the wooden plank that's sticking out (see Figure 13-13).**

Figure 13-13: Lampposts are cool ways to light up the night.

14

Ten Steps for Starting a Large-Scale Build

*Y*ou can build virtually anything in Minecraft, so why not use that ability to create impressive structures? This section lays out the steps you need to take to build exciting and creative structures.

Sketching Out a Rough Idea of the Structure

The first step to building a large-scale build is figuring out exactly what it is that you want to create. What's the building's purpose? What type of build is it? Is it large or small? What color should it be?

First, focus on the purpose of the building. How do you want to use it? Is it only for decoration, or does it have a function? For example, a library is for decoration, whereas a house serves a specific need. If your building is for decoration only, you don't have to think much about the purpose — you can focus on how the building will look. If your building has a specific function, think more about what you need to build or place inside and out (such as a furnace or a place to mine).

Though your building should look nice, the decorative aspect is secondary.

Where you decide to build contributes to your building's look. If you're building a library in the middle of a city, look at other structures in the city. For example, are they all square, or are they rounded? If all other structures are square, your library should be square, too — if it were rounded, it would look out of place. If you notice any other characteristics that the existing buildings have (such as a certain style of roof or a repeating color), use that same element in your building also so that it all fits together.

If you're unsure about which color best suits your building, consider its purpose (is it decorative or functional?), but also think about how you want it to look. For example, if you want your castle to look old and abandoned, use gray, cracked blocks, like cobblestone or moss stone, to build. If you want your building to look new and modern, use iron blocks or glowstone instead.

Selecting Blocks

Choosing blocks is simple: Just refer to your original plans and pick the type of block that matches the idea. For example, if you want your building to look ancient or abandoned, use cracked blocks that look like cracked stone bricks. If you want your building to look colorful and lively, use dyed wool. (Need to know more about dyed wool? Check out Chapters 5 and 11.)

If you didn't plan out the color of your building first, don't worry — doing so is easy. If you created the building with a specific theme, pick the color of the blocks based on that theme. If you built your structure to resemble a library instead, consider using bookshelves for the exterior blocks. If you're building a museum and you want it to look fancy on the outside, you can choose a block with a silver or tan color. For a more modern feel, on the other hand, choose blocks with a color that stands out, such as glowstone (gold) or purple wool (for purple).

As always, keep an eye on the surroundings of your new building. Most of the time, the new structure should blend in with its surroundings rather than stick out like a sore thumb. If you're in an evergreen forest, for example, a wooden plank house would fit in, but a sandstone house wouldn't, because that particular tan doesn't quite mesh with the greens and browns of the woods. (To see an example of a house that fits its surroundings and one that doesn't, check out the two structures shown in Figure 14-1.)

Figure 14-1: Buildings that fit — or don't fit — into their surroundings.

Setting Up Your Area

One thing we know is that setting up the area before you start building is a huge help — that little bit of prep work can often let you know whether you have enough room to build — and it can help you keep on track as you build.

To set up the area, you first need to *find* an area. Where do you want to be? On the beach? In the woods? In a city? But don't forget about the type of build you're starting — that aspect makes a difference in where you build. For example, a hospital in the middle of the woods doesn't look quite right. It makes more sense to place a hospital in a city.

After you find an area you like, start clearing it — you need an open space to build in. To clear an area, destroy any trees, grass, or flowers that are in your way. (To destroy blocks, left click the mouse button.)

As you clear the area, look to see whether you can spot any water or lava near you. If you do, find out where it's coming from, and try to stop the flow. The only reason that water might be helpful to you is if you want to build a farm. Other than that, the water will most likely just get in your way. If the water or lava is coming from a single hole in a mountain wall, place a single block in that hole to stop the flow.

Always ensure that your surroundings are safe — the last thing you want is to accidentally fall into a lava pool, for example.

Starting with a Central Room

After the area is cleared out and safe, it's time to start building! The best place to start is to build a central room, to serve as the hub of your build. It's the first room you enter, and you build all other rooms around it.

Building a central room is just like building any other room. First plan out the central room. Though this step may seem boring, don't skip it! Planning is vital because all the other rooms you build depend on the central room. If you build it and it's too large, you might run out of space quickly, and the other rooms you planned won't fit.

To determine the size of the central room, look at its original plans. How big are the other rooms supposed to be? How much room does that leave for your central room?

Any time you build, start with a *wireframe* (a block outline of your room; flip to Chapter 5 for a refresher) because it's easy to tear down or change. To build a wire frame, place the blocks on both sides for the length of the room, and then the width, so that you have a square (see Figure 14-2).

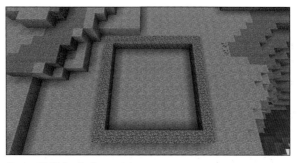

Figure 14-2: A wireframe base.

Next, make pillars in each corner of the wireframe base. However high you make the pillar is how tall the room will be. Figure 14-3 shows a wireframe with pillars.

Figure 14-3: The height of your building.

Finally, connect the top of the pillars to finish the wireframe for your room. Figure 14-4 shows a finished wireframe.

Figure 14-4: A finished wireframe.

Did you notice anything odd about the wireframe of the room? It has six holes: one above you, one below you, and four around you. Go ahead and fill in the holes with the block you want to build with. Now you have the central room! Don't worry that it's a little plain — we explain how to decorate it later in this chapter.

Wireframing the Rest of the Build

After you build the central room, you can wireframe the rest of your structure. Look at the original plans, and use wireframing blocks to make an outline of the rest of your build. Keep checking your plans so that you don't become confused or make a mistake. (If you do make a mistake, it's not the end of the world. That's one reason to wireframe — because you can easily fix and change things about your building!)

Filling in the Wireframe

To fill in the wireframe, place blocks inside it until it's full. To place a block, right-click. When the wireframe is filled, you end up with a wall. Keep filling in the wireframe until the outside of the structure is finished.

Remember the ceiling and the floor! To make these items, fill in the top and bottom of the wireframe, just like you filled in the sides.

If you're not happy about how your building looks on the outside, that's okay. We show you how to do some tweaking later.

Building within Your Structure

It's time for a tour! Enter your building and take a look around. It's pretty plain, right? Well, then, let's show you how to change the situation by decorating and adding some cool features.

If you have a theme in mind for your building or a specific purpose for it, start by adding items that fit your intentions. For example, if you built a house to live in, it needs some basic items, such as a furnace and a crafting table. (Refer to Chapters 1 and 4, if necessary.)

A house also needs light. A torch is a helpful light source, but you have other options, too. Glowstone not only looks good but also gives off a good amount of light. You can use redstone lamps, too. Or you can go with windows for natural light. (See Chapter 11 for more on windows.) If you truly want to get creative, build a glass ceiling — you'll always know what the weather's like!

Don't get too caught up in matching purpose and decorations. Just because your building has a purpose doesn't mean that you can't have fun items inside — it's okay to get creative. If you're decorating your house, for example, you can build bookcases, paintings, or stained glass items to add interest. (See Chapter 6 for more on these particular decorative touches.)

Don't stop with one room — decorate all your rooms! Later on, if you decide that you want to change the color of a wall or the decorations in a room, go ahead! Nothing is set in stone.

Don't Forget the Details

You have the outside finished. You have the inside finished. Now it's time to pay attention to the details. Elements such as trim (see Chapter 11), decorated doorways, and 3D designs can add pizazz to your build.

Trim makes the colors in your house stand out and helps your house look more three-dimensional (like a real-life house). Trim is all about the color of the blocks. Pick trim colors that complement each other. For example, wooden planks and nether brick go together well.

You can make the doorway stand out by adding some trim. Some people like to make their doors the same color as the trim, but you don't have to. The idea is to make sure that the door doesn't simply blend in with the wall. (Chapter 4 has more information about doorways.)

Finishing Up

You're so close! Your building is almost done; you have only a few, final touches remaining.

Go outside and look at your building. It's looking pretty cool, right? Even if it's looking good, you may see a component that looks somewhat odd or a place that needs sprucing up. No problem. If you see something you want to change, whether it's a major revision or a small tweak, go ahead and change it. That's the beauty of Minecraft — you can change anything at any time.

Be sure to look at your windows to see whether they match. Are they the same height? Are they the same number of blocks from each other? If not, and you want them to be more uniform, move them. Figure 14-5 shows even windows and uneven windows.

Figure 14-5: Even (left) and uneven (right) windows.

Another detail to examine is the door (or doors). At least once, we've built an item with a single door only to decide that we wanted a bigger one — so we built one. You can do this too by adding another door beside your first one (see Figure 14-6). When you do, the handles turn toward each other on their own.

When you're happy with the exterior details, take a look inside to see whether you want to change anything. If you do, go ahead and change it. This is your building, so it should look how you want it to look.

Figure 14-6: A fancy, two-door entrance.

One element that players sometimes want to change is the flooring. You can use just about anything for the floor. If you flip over to Chapter 11, you can find out how to make a lava or water floor. (Either one is cool!) But even block floors can be amazing — it all depends on the type of block you choose. Pick an interesting block such as nether brick or glowstone to make the floor look good. You can even add a pattern to the floor, as spelled out in Chapter 5.

Tweaking Your Building Constantly

Congratulations! You're pretty much finished with your building. Now you have only one last step to complete and that's to never stop making your building better. If you decide one day that you want more windows, go ahead and build more windows. Don't be afraid to make changes — you can always change them back if your revision doesn't work out, or you can make additional changes to make your building better.

Index